SpringerBriefs in Criminology

SpringerBriefs in Crime and Place

Series Editors
Joshua C. Hinkle
Georgia State University
Atlanta, Georgia, USA

Sue-Ming Yang
George Mason University
Fairfax, Virginia, USA

SpringerBriefs in Crime and Place presents concise summaries of cutting-edge research across the field of Crime and Place. It publishes small but impactful volumes of between 50-125 pages, with a clearly defined focus. The series covers a broad range of Crime and Place research, including: experimental design and advanced research methods, crime prevention, the role of communities and places, policy-related applications, and methodological issues in crime and place research at various units of analysis.

The scope of the series spans the whole field of Crime and Place, including the communities they are within, on the leading edge and advancing research. It is international and cross-disciplinary, including a broad array of topics, including the importance of the micro-place in research, policing, crime prevention, quantitative methods, experimental methods, research design and analysis, and crime prevention when considering a spatial perspective.

SpringerBriefs in Crime and Place will be of interest to a broad range of researchers and practitioners working in Crime and Place research and in related academic fields such as Sociology, Geography, Public Health, and Economics.

John E. Eck • Shannon J. Linning
Tamara D. Herold

Place Management and Crime

Ownership and Property Rights as a Source of Social Control

John E. Eck
School of Criminal Justice
University of Cincinnati
Cincinnati, OH, USA

Shannon J. Linning
School of Criminology
Simon Fraser University
Burnaby, BC, Canada

Tamara D. Herold
Department of Criminal Justice
University of Nevada, Las Vegas
Las Vegas, NV, USA

SpringerBriefs in Criminology
ISSN 2192-8533   ISSN 2192-8541 (electronic)
SpringerBriefs in Crime and Place
ISBN 978-3-031-27692-7   ISBN 978-3-031-27693-4 (eBook)
https://doi.org/10.1007/978-3-031-27693-4

© The Author(s), under exclusive license to Springer Nature Switzerland AG 2023
This work is subject to copyright. All rights are solely and exclusively licensed by the Publisher, whether the whole or part of the material is concerned, specifically the rights of translation, reprinting, reuse of illustrations, recitation, broadcasting, reproduction on microfilms or in any other physical way, and transmission or information storage and retrieval, electronic adaptation, computer software, or by similar or dissimilar methodology now known or hereafter developed.
The use of general descriptive names, registered names, trademarks, service marks, etc. in this publication does not imply, even in the absence of a specific statement, that such names are exempt from the relevant protective laws and regulations and therefore free for general use.
The publisher, the authors, and the editors are safe to assume that the advice and information in this book are believed to be true and accurate at the date of publication. Neither the publisher nor the authors or the editors give a warranty, expressed or implied, with respect to the material contained herein or for any errors or omissions that may have been made. The publisher remains neutral with regard to jurisdictional claims in published maps and institutional affiliations.

This Springer imprint is published by the registered company Springer Nature Switzerland AG
The registered company address is: Gewerbestrasse 11, 6330 Cham, Switzerland

About This Book

Why do a few addresses have so much crime but most places have so little? And what can we do about it? These are the questions we tackle in this book. The theory, evidence, and practices we discuss developed over 30 years, beginning in the early 1990s. The theory, evidence, and practices were the result of many collaborations among academics, police officials, and community members. In the process, our research led new crime reduction strategies and made us question some basic ideas in criminology.

This book is the first all-encompassing description of place management theory and practice. It is the prequel to our earlier work, *Whose 'Eyes on the Street' Control Crime? Expanding Place Management into Neighborhoods.* In that book, we show how place management creates safe or unsafe areas within cities. It begins where this book ends. The people who own and operate places are the subject of this book.

We designed this book for a broad audience. Students and their instructors should find it useful for exploring the criminology of place and challenging community criminology. Activist readers, those in communities or government agencies, interested in doing something about crime, will find our book useful for developing crime reduction strategies.

We strived to make our ideas clear and readable to a wide audience, not just academic researchers. We use tables showing the relationships among studies and theory. We use figures to diagram our ideas. And we use photographs of places to give readers a gut sense of the range of places we are discussing.

The study and application of place management theory is ongoing. We mark the topics where the social science evidence is extremely strong. And we mark where the evidence is modest or weak, contradictory, or absent. As much as we have learned over the last three decades, there is much yet to learn.

"Power follows property."
John Adams, Charles Beard, Sir John Dalrymple, Aldous Huxley, James Madison, Daniel Webster, and maybe more. Others have implied the same sentiment, but with more words. All are following James Harrington, *The Commonwealth of Oceana* (1656).

We hope our book gives you sharp probing questions you can use to forge useful ways to reduce crime. We urge you to collect data and evidence about the successes of your efforts, and pass what you learned to others so they can learn. Much of what we learned, we learned from practitioners who shared their successes and failures. We hope you do the same.

Acknowledgments

We give a hearty shout-out to Police Chief Maris Herold of the Boulder Police Department. Not only is she married to one of us, she has been a stalwart supporter of crime-place research, a perceptive advice giver, and an inspirational innovator. We would follow her into any place.

As always, many thanks to Charlotte Navarro, who provided amazingly perceptive comments.

We also give our heartfelt thanks to our editors, Dr. Sue-Ming Yang and Dr. Josh Hinkle. They enthusiastically embraced our idea for this book and gave us great advice.

Contents

1	**Places and Crime**.	1
	Social Control Hidden in Plain Sight	1
	Place, Place Managers, and Place Management.	2
	The Concentration of Crime at Places	3
	The Argument That Follows	8
	References.	9
2	**Why Some Places Are Bad**	11
	Explanation 0: It's Random	11
	Explanation 1: Reporting Bias	13
	Explanation 2: Size Matters	13
	Explanation 3: Repeat Victimization	14
	Explanation 4: Hot Products.	14
	Explanation 5: Offender Concentration	15
	Explanation 6: Repeat Offenders	15
	Explanation 7: Inadequate Guardianship	16
	Explanation 8: Poor Handling.	16
	Explanation 9: Low Informal Social Control	17
	Explanation 10: Bad Physical Design.	17
	Too Many Explanations	18
	Appendix: Three Explanations for Proximal Place Crime Concentration.	19
	References.	20
3	**Place Management**	23
	Place Managers.	23
	The Four Functions of Place Management.	24
	Organization of Space.	25
	Regulation of Conduct	26
	Control of Access	26
	Acquisition of Resources	27
	Place Management as a Keystone Explanation.	27

		Organization of Space...............................	28
		Regulation of Conduct	28
		Control of Access	29
		Acquisition of Resources	29
	Crime Prevention Within Places...........................		29
		Situational Crime Prevention	29
		Evidence Situational Prevention Works at Places......	30
	Conclusions...		31
	References..		32
4	**Sources of Powers**		33
	Being Explicit About Sources of Control Powers...........		33
	Defining Forms of Control		33
	What Is Community Informal Social Control?...............		34
		X: Actors..	34
		A: Actions...	35
		T: Targets...	35
		G: Goals	35
		P: Powers..	36
	The Source of Power of Place Managers		36
		Property Rights....................................	37
		Rights That May Be Included in a Bundle of Rights ..	38
	Authority, Power, and Social Control		41
	References..		43
5	**Place Manager Failures and Successes**		45
	Why Some Fail But Most Do Not...........................		45
	Controls on Place Managers..............................		45
	Failures		48
	Conclusions...		52
	References..		53
6	**The Extended Place Manager I: Crime Radiation**		55
	Introduction...		55
	Do Some Facilities Radiate Crime to Their Purlieus?		56
	The Diffusion of Crime Control Benefits and Its Implications.......		61
	Direct Evidence for Radiation		62
	Conclusions...		63
	References..		64
7	**The Extended Place Manager II: Hidden Crime-Involved Places and Place Networks**.....................		67
	Introduction...		67
	Place Types and Crime Functions.........................		68
		Crime Sites	69
		Convergence Settings	69
		Comfort Spaces....................................	70

	Corrupting Spots.	70
	Networked Places and Violent Crime Hot Spots	71
	Tackling Crime-Involved Place Networks	73
	Place Network Investigations (PNI)	74
	Place Network Investigations Evidence	75
	Conclusions.	76
	References.	77
8	**The Extended Place Manager III: Place Networks for Safety**	79
	Jane Jacobs' *Eyes on the Street*.	79
	Jane Jacobs' *Constant Succession of Eyes*	80
	How Place Managers Expand Their Control	82
	Implications.	86
	References.	87
9	**Reducing Crime at High-Crime Places**.	89
	The Limits of Hot Spots Patrols	89
	The Advantages of Problem-Oriented Policing	91
	The Centrality of Regulation	93
	Regulating the Means for Reducing Crime	93
	Regulating the Ends of Crime Prevention.	94
	A Comprehensive Place-Based Strategy.	97
	References.	98
10	**Rethinking the Forms of Social Control**.	101
	Thinking About Crime and Its Control.	101
	The Problems of Neighborhood Thinking	102
	Forms of Control.	106
	State Control.	107
	Place Management	107
	Self-Control.	108
	Interpersonal Control	108
	Overlaps and Layers	108
	Four Questions	109
	References.	110
Index.		113

About the Authors

John E. Eck has worked on ways to improve policing, particularly criminal investigations management and problem-oriented policing, since 1977. While assisting police with their problem-solving efforts, he became fascinated with crime places. He created the idea of place management during his work with the San Diego Police Department and while writing his doctoral dissertation. This led to his spending over 25 years developing the implications of place management for crime prevention, often in vital collaboration with current and former graduate students. He is a professor in the School of Criminal Justice within the University of Cincinnati, author of *Writing with Sweet Clarity*, and second author of *Whose 'Eyes on the Street' Control Crime? Expanding Place Management into Neighborhoods*.

Shannon J. Linning is an assistant professor in the School of Criminology at Simon Fraser University in Vancouver, Canada. She earned her doctorate in criminal justice with an emphasis in crime prevention from the University of Cincinnati. Her research examines how we can reduce crime at places by partnering with those in property development, business, real estate, and urban planning. Her work is published in various peer-reviewed journals. Her newest book, *Whose 'Eyes on the Street' Control Crime? Expanding Place Management into Neighborhoods*, has been nominated for the Michael J. Hindelang Outstanding Book Award through the American Society of Criminology.

Tamara D. Herold is an associate professor of Criminal Justice at the University of Nevada, Las Vegas. She uses the crime science perspective to study the criminological impact of the design and management of places, as well as crowd and neighborhood dynamics associated with violence. She defined the process of place management while earning her doctorate at the University of Cincinnati, under the direction of John E. Eck. She develops and evaluates place-based crime reduction strategies for police agencies, and she is the architect of the Place Network Investigations violence reduction initiative, which received the 2017 Herman Goldstein Award for Problem-Oriented Policing.

Chapter 1
Places and Crime

Social Control Hidden in Plain Sight

Control requires power. The control of mischief and mischief-makers is not an exception. Power may come from a bond between the mischief-maker and a parent. Or power comes from the state. But come power must. This book is about power and control of the serious mischief called crime. It is about a specific source of power and control. The source is so common, so mundane, so unexceptional, and so obvious that you probably do not notice it. If you notice it, you probably do not see its significance. Like you, policy makers and crime researchers usually overlook this source of control. This source of control is *place management*. It may be among the most powerful sources of crime control we have.

Why is the failure to notice and attend to place management important? Because when people attend to place management, they can usually reduce crime. And because when policy makers fail to address place management, their policies are unsustainable, usually costly, and frequently ineffective.

The facts are these. Crime is concentrated at a very small proportion of addresses. Most addresses in any neighborhood have little or no crime. A few addresses, in any neighborhood, have a great deal of crime. There are many explanations for these two facts; all involve the way owners and operators use their property rights to manage their places. Most place managers exercise their property rights in ways that keep their places safe. Public policy should build on these successes. A few place managers fail persistently. These few persistent failures create much of the crime neighborhoods experience. To control crime, public policy must reverse these routine failures.

Policy makers and researchers must throw off their bipolar notions of social control. Safety is not created just by police or just by community residents or by some combination. Place managers exercise considerable control over people's behaviors. And place managers are not police and they often are not residents. Their influence can extend beyond their property into surrounding areas. Understanding place management reveals effective crime control strategies that can reduce the use of criminal sanctions, strategies with teeth so the police do not have to bite as often or as hard.

In this book, we provide answers to four questions: (1) *Where* precisely is crime the highest? (2) *Who* owns or operates these places? (3) *How* do their management practices create crime opportunities? (4) *What* can be done to get the managers of these few crime-prone places to change their practices so that crime declines? In the pages that follow, we explain what we mean by these questions, show why these questions are important, and review the evidence for their answers. Demonstrating the importance of these questions requires us to contrast our management perspective with the neighborhood, or community, perspective.

But first you need to understand what we mean by the word *place*. We then turn to the fact that crime is concentrated at a tiny fraction of places. Crime concentration is the rock upon which our arguments rest. The third section of our introduction outlines the nine-chapter argument that makes up this book.

Place, Place Managers, and Place Management

What is a *place*? To some people it means a large area: neighborhood or city. Not to us. To some people it means a block or street segment. Not to us. To us, a place is a property parcel, often labeled by an address or the name of a business or organization. There is nothing wrong with the other uses for this word. But they are not our uses. So we make these distinctions so none of us will be confused.

We call our type of place a *proprietary place*. Proprietary places have three required characteristics and two common characteristics.

Location We can find a proprietary place on a map. This is a necessary condition. We can represent a proprietary place as a dot. The dot is usually fixed but some places move: busses, planes, trains, and ships are examples of mobile places. Think of them as a string of dots. In short, a proprietary place is not a state of mind (like *community*): you can go there and see it.

Boundary A proprietary place has a shape with defined borders. This too is a necessary condition. Legal documents codify a proprietary place's bounds. The legal power to regulate behavior at the place end at the boundary. Many other geographic entities do not have clear boundaries—neighborhoods, for example—and their fuzzy boundaries do not define the limits of control.

Owned A proprietary place has an owner. Ownership is a necessary condition for something to be a proprietary place also. A single-family home is owned by the homeowner. A place of worship is owned by its members or a larger religious institution. An apartment building is owned by a landlord, a property management company, or other entity. A government building is owned by a government. Nonproprietary places, such as street segments and neighborhoods, have many owners usually.

These three necessary conditions produce two common characteristics of proprietary places.

Function Often proprietary places have a single dominant function. Houses and apartments are for long-term living. A motel is for short-term living. A bar is for drinking. A park is for recreation. Sometimes a proprietary place has multiple functions: a building with shops on the ground floor, parking on the second and third floors, and apartments above that; a church that has services for several hours out of the week, serves as a soup kitchen for other hours, and a place for adult education at other times; and a park for children to play, for strollers to enjoy the outdoors, and for evening concerts.

Small A proprietary place is a very small place, usually. Many fit into a street block and hundreds fit into a neighborhood. By small we mean its physical footprint on the ground. A 20-story apartment building may contain more people than most city blocks, but it contains them on a small land parcel. A few proprietary places may be large: a shopping mall, factory, or airport are examples.

A *place manager* is a person who owns a proprietary place or is someone to whom the owner has delegated authority to operate a place. We explain this later. For now, we only need to state that ownership carries legally enforceable rights over a place and owners can delegate some of these rights. *Place management* is what place managers do to operate the place and carry out its functions. This too, we will expand upon later.

Whenever you read *place* in this book, you should think of a small owned parcel of land with a function. We will not always use the adjective *proprietary*, but when we do it is to highlight the differences in meaning between our use of the word and the uses by others.

The Concentration of Crime at Places

There are three laws of criminology. First, young people—roughly from age 15 through 25—create most of the trouble. Second, males cause more trouble than females regardless of age. Third, crime is highly concentrated at a few places (Weisburd, 2015). This means that even within high-crime areas, like neighborhoods, only a tiny number of places experience crime. There are no known exceptions to this law, unlike the first two laws. Failing to detect any exceptions has been a powerful discovery.

Charles Booth was the first to connect proprietary places to crime in his maps of London (LSE Library, 2016; Morgan & Sinclair, 2019). He classified addresses by

W.E.B. Du Bois's full map shows property parcels inhabited by African Americans, color-coded by class. We are interested in crime, not class, so we show African-American parcels in grey, with the exception of class 4, "The lowest class of criminals, prostitutes and loafers; the submerged class" (Du Bois, 1973, pp310-11), which are in black. White parcels are either white residences, businesses, or public buildings.

Du Bois's map illustrates his understanding of the way crime concentrates at the parcel level. It shows the 26 crime parcels scatter among the many non-crime parcels. With the rise of neighborhood theories of crime, Du Bois's insights were lost and entire areas were labeled crime prone.

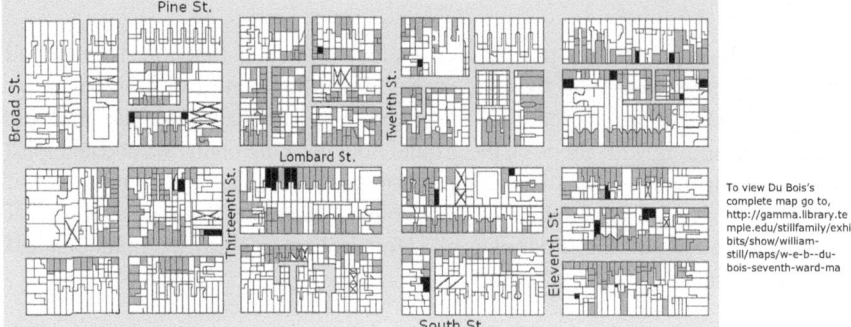

To view Du Bois's complete map go to, http://gamma.library.temple.edu/stillfamily/exhibits/show/william-still/maps/w-e-b--du-bois-seventh-ward-ma

Fig. 1.1 Crime, place, and W.E.B. Du Bois

the social class of the residents, with the bottom class being "Lowest class. Vicious, semi-criminal." W.E.B Du Bois (1973 [1899]) applied Booth's methods to an African-American ward in Philadelphia. We show a portion of Du Bois' map in Fig. 1.1, with buildings inhabited by "Grade 4 Vicious and Criminal Classes" shaded in black. Du Bois showed that, contrary to popular belief, the vast majority of the seventh ward was middle class, working class, or poor, not criminal.

If analyzed by an early twenty-first-century neighborhood-crime researcher, the researcher would mark the entire area as high crime. A twenty-first-century crime analyst would single out the Lombard Street segment, between 13th and 12th streets, as a crime hot spot. Crime-place researchers, like us, focus on 4 parcels (out of 42) on Lombard Street.

Social research in the nineteenth and early twentieth centuries often focused on addresses. John Snow's London cholera maps of 1854 showed the number of cholera victims at each address (Johnson, 2006). Florence Kelly and colleagues at Hull House mapped housing conditions by building in Chicago (Residents of Hull House, 1895), as did Robert Hunter (1901) 6 years later. Sadly, place-level studies faded as area-level analysis became popular (Shaw & McKay, 1972). The result was that residents took on the reputations of the areas defined by government agencies, business interests, and researchers. Du Bois, by contrast, insisted on showing that the reputation of the area masked the characteristics of the residents.

After Du Bois, it took 90 years for criminologists to return to proprietary places. Researchers in Minneapolis (Sherman et al., 1989) and Boston (Pierce et al., 1988) pick up where Du Bois left off, but with modern analytical tools. They showed that crime and disorder were concentrated at a relatively few high-crime addresses. In Minneapolis, half of a city's crime occurred at only 3.3% of its addresses. Regardless of the neighborhood examined, researchers found that most addresses and street corners had little or no crime. And in all neighborhoods, a very few places had a great deal of crime. As Du Bois (and Booth) had pointed out, and criminologists forgot, neighborhoods are not generally criminogenic. It is high-crime parcels that drive crime and give areas their reputations (Eck, 2019).

Around a decade later, David Weisburd and colleagues (2004, 2013) demonstrated that crime accumulated along a relatively few street segments, leaving most street segments relatively, if not completely, crime-free. Segments behaved the same in high- and low-crime areas. This is exactly the same distribution of crime found among Boston and Minneapolis addresses. A street segment is not a proprietary place, however. A street segment is a *proximal place*. These "are small groups of proprietary places clustered close in space" (Madensen & Eck, 2013, p. 558). Madensen and Eck (2013) refer to larger areas, such as neighborhoods, as *pooled places*. These are groups of proximal places.

We can see these different types of places in Fig. 1.1. The proprietary places are the parcels lining the streets and alleys. Proximal places are segments of streets. Lombard between Thirteenth and Twelfth streets is an example. There are at least 42 proprietary places directly on this segment. The Seventh Ward (only a portion of which we show in Fig. 1.1) is a single pooled place. It has about 142 square blocks (when we ignore alleys) and approximately 315 street segments. One square block contains a hospital. This is the only proprietary place that is also a proximal place.

Table 1.1 summarizes the typical characteristics of these three place types. A point on a map can represent a proprietary place, though on a large-scale map, the shape of the property parcel becomes visible.

Proximal places can be represented as short lines or thin rectangles. Proximal places have relatively clear boundaries because the street layout provides clear markings.

Pooled places cover large areas. Any two-dimensional shape can depict them. Residents often disagree about neighborhood boundaries (Burdick-Will, 2018;

Table 1.1 Comparison of place types

	Place type		
	Proprietary	Proximal	Pooled
Location	A point	A line or very thin rectangle	A large two-dimensional shape
Boundary	Defined by property deed	Defined by street intersections	Defined by government or business
Single owner	Yes, with some exceptions	Seldom	Almost never
Function	One or a few	Many	Large number
Size	Tiny	Small	Large
Common terms	House, building, parcel, address	Street segment, street block	Neighborhood, community, district, ward, precinct, tract
Pioneering crime research	Booth (1893) Du Bois (1899) Sherman et al. (1989)	Weisburd et al. (2004) Weisburd et al. (2013)	Park et al. (1925) Shaw and McKay (1972)

Suttles, 1972; Venkatesh, 2001). But the bureaucracies that created these areas—school officials, postal service workers, police, census takers, city planners, and sanitation workers, for example—usually know the boundaries of their work areas. In the private sector, real estate agents may be very aware of these boundaries. We return to the ambiguity of pooled places in our last chapter.

The heterogeneity of ownership increases from proprietary to pooled places. Typically, a proprietary place has a single owner, though there are some notable exceptions. A high-rise condominium has many owners, for example. Usually, no single owner possesses a proximal place, though we noted an exception in Du Boise's map: a hospital. A pooled place has many owners, some are residents, but some owners live elsewhere; they rent or lease their properties.

A proprietary place often has a single dominant function or a very few functions. A residential street block has two functions: providing homes and facilitating movement along streets and sidewalks. Many proximal places, particularly in urban cores, contain a variety of functions: shopping, recreation, residential, mobility, and even manufacturing. Functional variation within pooled places is even greater.

The variation in size is pronounced and obvious. Within urban areas (and outside rural agricultural areas), land parcels are tiny. Segments and blocks are many times larger. And areas larger still.

Place types

A **proprietary place**: a corner bar, with apartments above.

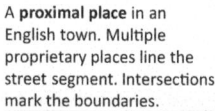

A **proximal place** in an English town. Multiple proprietary places line the street segment. Intersections mark the boundaries.

A **pooled place**: a neighborhood, in Cincinnati, United States. It contains many street segments, and hundreds of proprietary places. The official neighborhood boundary runs along the tree line, just beyond the steeple at the top.

These distinctions are important for understanding crime. If you assume that a neighborhood is the right unit, you are assuming the processes that create crime operate throughout the neighborhood; they permeate all blocks, segments, and parcels. So the distribution of crime should be reasonably even. If you assume that a street segment is the right unit, you are assuming that crime processes run the length of the segment and permeate parcels on each side of the street.

Weisburd and colleagues (2004) pointed out that within neighborhoods, adjacent street segments can display big differences in crime levels. Neighborhoods have considerable heterogeneity in the distribution of crime. Calling an area a "high-crime neighborhood" is misleading. By demonstrating the variability of crime among street segments in the same neighborhood, Weisburd's team substantially undercut our confidence that neighborhood theories of crime are useful.

By 2015, there were many studies of crime concentration at addresses and street segments. In a meta-analysis of these studies, YongJei Lee and associates (2017) showed that the concentration of crime at proprietary and proximal places was extremely common. In a subsequent study, Lee (2017) showed most addresses in high-crime street segments were crime-free. A few street segments were crime prone entire their length, but such segments were rare. Lee's work suggests that even within street segments, crime variability is more common than similarity.

Further evidence for the primacy of proprietary places comes from risky facilities studies (Eck et al., 2007). In Sherman and company's (1989) research, the authors examined crime in general and multiple types of crime. They did not investigate the hypothesis that concentration might be due to crime concentrating at a few types of places: bars, for example. Eck, Clarke, and Guerette (2007) call places of a single type a *facility*. They showed that a few places within a given facility type drive crime. Madensen and Eck (2008) found this is true of drinking places. Studying every bar in Cincinnati, Ohio, they found that most bars (62%) had no violent incidents during their 2-year study period. But a few bars (20%) experienced most of (75%) the violence. Just as a few high-crime places give a neighborhood a bad reputation, a few bars give all bars a bad reputation. What is true of Cincinnati bars turns out to be true of all types of facilities. This is true of places of worship, schools, bus stops, and every other facility examined (Eck et al., 2007; Wilcox & Eck, 2011). In short, crime follows the same distribution found in Minneapolis and Boston even when looking at one type of facility. There is no known exception.

So why would land uses be correlated with high-crime levels? There are two possible reasons for this. One is that most facilities examined are commercial and they are located on busy streets. Thus, it is not the facility type but the traffic moving past them that matters (Tillyer & Walter, 2019; Wilcox & Eck, 2011). Traffic is a characteristic of proximal places, like street segments.

Another possibility is that those extremely crime-prone facilities—the riskiest facilities—are created by poor management. We will closely examine this theory and the evidence behind it in the following chapters.

In the next chapter, we will dig deeper into the causes of high crime at a few proprietary places. But before examining causes, we should summarize the research we have just described.

Figure 1.2 is a generic diagram of how proprietary (and proximal) places are associated with crime. It summarizes 45 years of crime-place research (Eck et al., 2007; Lee et al., 2017). As we have emphasized, the statistical shape appears to be universal and to resemble a hockey stick: the handle begins at the far left and continues to the upward blade on the right. The hockey stick shape appears regardless of the crime type examined, as long as there are enough crimes to produce a reliable shape. A hockey stick appears regardless of the type of facility examined, as long as

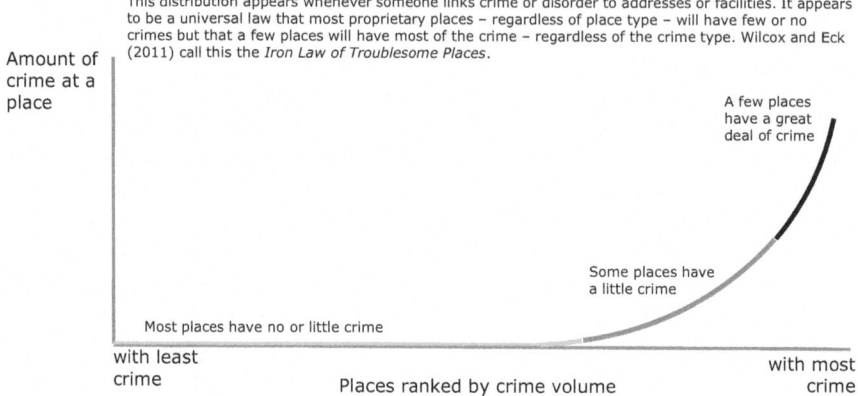

Fig. 1.2 The hockey stick curve of crime concentration. (See Wilcox and Eck (2011))

there are enough facilities of that type to produce a reliable curve. The hockey stick appears every time an analyst plots crime at proprietary places, without exception.

The hockey stick in Fig. 1.2 suggests that to understand crime we need to look at areas much smaller than neighborhoods. It suggests we need to explore what is going on in the few places with a great deal of trouble—those in the blade of the stick—compared to most places with little or no trouble, those in the handle. It suggests that crime control efforts should be hyper-focused on the blade rather than spread over the handle. Moreover, the hockey stick implies we should think about who owns the relatively few places in the blade. They may help us control crime.

The Argument That Follows

In the chapters that follow, we pursue the implications we just listed. The next chapter investigates the many reasons why some proprietary places are troublesome but most are not. In Chap. 3, we show how all these explanations point to place management. Place managers control place users' behaviors, but to exercise this control, they need power. The source of that power is the subject of our fourth chapter. Power explains why place managers can and do control crime, but we need to know why they sometimes fail. Chap. 5 explains these failures. Chapters 6, 7, and 8 show that the influences of place management extend beyond parcels to nearby places, down street segments, and into neighborhoods. Our ninth chapter describes how local governments can control place-based crime, given the lessons from earlier chapters. In our final chapter, we challenge criminologist's narrow view of how people control crime. We show that expanding our thinking on who controls crime provides a richer array of crime-fighting options.

References

Booth, C. (1893). Life and labour of the people of London: First results of an inquiry based on the 1891 census. *Journal of the Royal Statistical Society, 56*(4), 557–593.

Burdick-Will, J. (2018). School location, social ties, and perceived neighborhood boundaries. *City & Community, 17*(2), 418–437.

Du Bois, W. E. B (1973) [1899]. *The Philadelphia Negro*. Kraus-Thomson Organization.

Eck, J. E. (2019). Race, place management, and crime. In J. D. Unnever, S. L. Gabbidon, & C. Chouhy (eds.), *Building a black criminology: Race, theory, and crime* (pp.171–206). Routledge.

Eck, J. E., Clarke, R. V., & Guerette, R. T. (2007). Risky facilities: Crime concentration in homogeneous sets of establishments and facilities. In G. Farrell, K. J. Bowers, S. D. Johnson, & M. Townsley (Eds.), *Imagination for crime prevention: Essays in honour of Ken Pease* (pp. 225–264). Criminal Justice Press.

Hunter, R. (2018) [1901]. *Tenement conditions in Chicago: Report by the investigating Committee of the City Homes Association*. Forgotten Books. https://www.forgottenbooks.com/en/books/TenementConditionsinChicago_10660275.

Johnson, S. (2006). *The ghost map: The story of London's most terrifying epidemic--and how it changed science, cities, and the modern world*. Riverhead Books.

Lee, Y. (2017). *Comparing measures of the concentration of crime at places and times*. Unpublished dissertation, University of Cincinnati.

Lee, Y., Eck, J. E., O, S.-H., & Martinez, N. N. (2017). How concentrated is crime at places? A systematic review from 1970 to 2015. *Crime Science, 6*(1). https://doi.org/10.1186/s40163-017-0069-x

LSE Library. (2016). *Charles Booth's London: Poverty maps and police notebooks*. London School of Economics & Political Science. https://booth.lse.ac.uk/. Accessed 5 Oct 2022.

Madensen, T. D., & Eck, J. E. (2008). Violence in bars: Exploring the impact of place manager decision-making. *Crime Prevention and Community Safety, 10*, 111–125.

Madensen, T. D., & Eck, J. E. (2013). Crime places and place management. In F. T. Cullen & P. Wilcox (Eds.), *The Oxford handbook of criminological theory* (pp. 554–578). Oxford University Press.

Morgan, M. S., & Sinclair, I. (2019). *Charles Booth's London poverty maps*. Thames & Hudson.

Park, R. E., Burgess, E., & McKenzie, R. (1925). *The City*. University of Chicago Press.

Pierce, G., Spaar, S., & Briggs, L. R. (1988). *The character of police work: Strategic and tactical implications*. Center for Applied Social Research, Northeastern University.

Residents of Hull-House. (1895). *Hull-house maps and papers: A presentation of nationalities and wages in a congested district of Chicago, together with comments and essays on problems growing out of social conditions*. Thomas Y. Crowell.

Shaw, C. R., & McKay, H. D. (1972). *Juvenile delinquency and urban areas* (Revised ed.). University of Chicago Press.

Sherman, L. W., Gartin, P. R., & Buerger, M. E. (1989). Hot spots of predatory crime: Routine activities and the criminology of place. *Criminology, 27*(1), 27–55.

Suttles, G. (1972). *The social construction of communities*. University of Chicago Press.

Tillyer, M. S., & Walter, R. J. (2019). Busy businesses and busy contexts: The distribution and sources of crime at commercial properties. *Journal of Research in Crime and Delinquency, 56*(6), 816–850.

Venkatesh, S. (2001). Chicago's pragmatic planners. *Social Science History, 2*(summer), 275–317.

Weisburd, D. (2015). The law of crime concentration and the criminology of place. *Criminology, 53*(2), 133–157.

Weisburd, D., Bushway, S., Lum, C., & Yang, S.-M. (2004). Crime trajectories at places: A longitudinal study of street segments in the city of Seattle. *Criminology, 42*(2), 283–322.

Weisburd, D., Groff, E. R., & Yang, S.-M. (2013). *The criminology of place: Street segments and our understanding of the crime problem*. Oxford University Press.

Wilcox, P., & Eck, J. E. (2011). Criminology of the unpopular. *Criminology & Public Policy, 10*(2), 473–482.

Chapter 2
Why Some Places Are Bad

In the previous chapter, we showed that crime is extremely concentrated at very few small places. In this chapter, we dig into explanations for this concentration of crime at proprietary places. We describe ten explanations for crime concentration at places. These cover all explanations we have found in the research literature, plus a few that researchers have not given but can be inferred from routine activity and other theories (Felson, 2016).

The crime triangle, shown in Fig. 2.1, shows the principle elements of routine activity theory. The core idea of routine activity theory is that crime is likely when the routines of offenders (those who initiate deviance) and targets (possible victims and desirable things) converge at a place where controls on behavior are lax.

Offenders, targets, and places are shown on the inner triangle. Their convergence is necessary for crime. Controllers are shown on the outer triangle. Guardians protect people, things, and animals that offenders want to attack, take, or damage. Handlers deter potential offender misbehavior by threatening withdrawal of emotional support. Managers govern places. We will discuss each of these controllers in greater depth later. From this diagram, we develop at least ten explanations for the hockey stick distribution of crime.

But ten explanations are too many. So by the end of the chapter, we are poised to dive into place management, the topic of Chap. 3.

Explanation 0: It's Random

This is not an explanation for crime concentration. It is an explanation for why we think there is systematic concentration when there is not. We know that a random process can give rise to patterns that appear meaningful—seeing the face of your childhood dog in the clouds or believing your luck is due to seeing your deceased dog's image. If you flip a coin many times, you will see runs of heads or tails or even

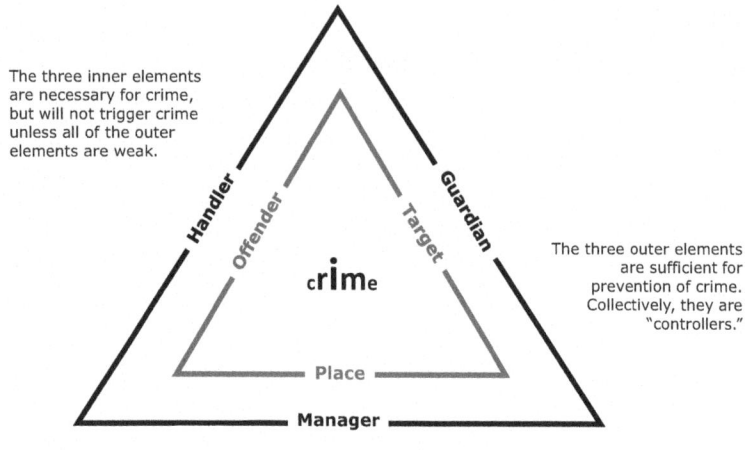

Fig. 2.1 Routine activity theory's triangles (See Clarke & Eck (2003))

runs of heads-tails and more complex patterns. Perhaps, the concentration Sherman and colleagues (1989) discovered in Minneapolis is the product of such randomness.

Fortunately, Sherman's team tested for randomness. They compared the distribution of crimes across places to the distribution of crimes that would occur if randomness were the cause. If the two distributions looked similar, then they would have concluded that some arbitrary process was at work. Instead, they found that the actual and the random distributions looked very different. Thus, they rejected the notion that randomness created crime concentration at places. Many subsequent studies of crime at places did not conducted such tests, but the few that did came to the same conclusion as Sherman and company (1989).

There is another reason for rejecting the random explanation. If crime were randomly popping up in places, then this year's high-crime location would be different from last year's. Similarly, having no crime at a place this year would not predict no crime in previous or subsequent years. In short, crime across places would be highly erratic.

It is not erratic, however. Research into crime stability at both proximal and proprietary places shows stability (Andresen et al., 2017a, 2017b; Andresen & Malleson, 2011; Braga et al., 2010, 2011; Groff et al., 2010; Payne & Gallagher, 2016; Spelman, 1995; Steenbeek & Weisburd, 2016; Walter et al., 2022; Wenger & Lantz, 2022; Weisburd et al., 2004, 2009). There is some year-to-year change but not the level of change we would see if a random process was at work.

So let's set this non-explanation aside and look at systematic reasons a few places may have more crime than others.

Explanation 1: Reporting Bias

When we count crimes at places, we usually count crimes reported to the police. Therefore, we must consider the possibility that what is concentrating at a few places are reporting behaviors rather than crime. Consider this extreme example. We observe 100 hair salons and count reported crime at each. We discover that 5 salons report 70 percent of the crimes at salons, and 50 salons report no crime. Then we conduct a survey of all salons and find that when we ask salon owners, they have about the same number of crimes. However, most salon owners do not report the crimes and discourage their customers from reporting. What about the five salons that seem to have a great deal of crime? Their owners report all crimes and encourage their customers to do the same.

Reporting bias does occur. For example, John once interviewed a police officer who described her investigation of a troublesome location that was the result of a store clerk calling the police whenever he was fearful. Magnet phones, used before most people carried mobile phones, provides another example. As Buerger et al. (1995: p. 250) describe:

> "Magnet phones" were usually pay phones at convenience stores, gas stations and other locations. ... Persons needing the police would go to these public locations, often up to six blocks away, to call 911. Because they waited to meet the police at the phone, the place ... was registered as the address where the phone was located in the "address" line of the dispatch record.

However, there are no systematic studies showing that at a few places, almost all crimes are reported (thus showing up in the blade of the hockey stick), but at most places almost all crimes go unreported to the police. Further, if such reporting practices were common, then all of us would experience far more crime than we do as all the places we think of as safe would be dangerous. Reporting bias should be considered when examining a specific place, but is extremely unlikely to be a general explanation.

Explanation 2: Size Matters

Maybe very high-crime locations are larger, have more people using them, and thus have more targets. A large store will have more customers and more things to steal, so it will have more reports of shoplifting than a small store selling the same things. Patricia and Paul Brantingham (1995) called such places *crime generators*.

Size does matter, but not always. When the Chula Vista Police examined calls to the police from motels, for example, they looked at the number of calls per room per year at each motel. Looking at crime per room controlled for the size of the motel. A few highly troublesome motels still stood out from the norm (Bichler et al., 2013). In a study by the Boulder Colorado Police, controlling for size did not substantially change the conclusion that a few fraternity and sorority houses contributed to most of the trouble at these facilities (Wartell et al., 2021). In a study of bag thefts in bars in London, British researchers used the number of seats in each bar as an indicator of size. They found no association between number of seats bars and their number of bag thefts (Sidebottom & Bowers, 2010). Size may thwart some crimes. When studying where drug dealers set up shop, Eck (1994) found that they were more likely to choose small apartment buildings over larger ones.

Size is something to attend to but it is not a universal rule. Even when size does contribute to the disparity in crime levels, one has to ask, why some facilities are bigger than others; size is under the control of the people who own the place.

Explanation 3: Repeat Victimization

A place may have high-crime levels if it is frequented by a few repeat victims. Most people are not victimized by crime, but some people are repeat victims (Grove et al., 2012), and repeat victimization has been documented in many studies in many countries (O et al., 2017). In fact, the distribution of crimes over potential victims is quite similar to the distribution of crimes over places (Eck et al., 2017). It too looks like a hockey stick. So perhaps it's not the place, but the victim.

Repeat victimization is often confused with repeated crimes at places because the repeat victimization literature overlaps with the repeat place research (Farrell & Sousa, 1998; Farrell, 2015). The earliest studies of repeat victimization dealt with experiences with burglaries, crimes against places (Polvi et al., 1991). Therefore, one could define repeated crimes at places as a form of repeat victimization. The drawback to this is that it blinds one to the role of those who operate places. Treating repeated robberies of the same bank is fundamentally different from treating repeated assaults on the same person at different addresses. So although repeat victimization can make a contribution to understanding concentration of some crimes at particular addresses, it is unlikely to be a general explanation.

Explanation 4: Hot Products

When the offenders' targets are things rather than people, it is useful to examine which products are stolen and which are not. As Clarke (1999) declared, some products are hot. In particular, things that a thief can conceal, easily remove, find handily, values highly, enjoys using, and can dispose of quickly will be stolen more often than items that do not have these characteristics (Clarke, 1999). Offenders are more likely to steal iPhones than toilets, for example. If one were studying retail facilities, it is possible that the relatively few high-theft stores stock more hot products than the numerous low-theft stores.

Here again, we have a plausible explanation for some high-crime places, but not an explanation that can be generalized. For one thing, it does not explain concentrations of violence. Nor does it explain concentrations of crime when the targets are relatively homogeneous; bank robbers inevitably take cash, for example. Cash from one bank is just as useful as cash from another, yet bank robberies follow the hockey stick distribution (Matthews et al., 2001).

Explanation 5: Offender Concentration

Let's turn to offenders. The first of the offender explanations is that a few places have a lot of them, and most places have few. It is doubtful that offenders spread themselves evenly across places. And a few places must have many offenders, a gang clubhouse, for example. So if a place attracts many offenders, it is likely to have a great deal of crime relative to the places to which offenders avoid. The Brantinghams (1995) called these types of locations *crime attractors*.

One of the problems with crime attractors is that they are likely to become police and private security attractors. If misbehaving offenders can be routinely found at a place and the misbehavior creates trouble for those who control a location, those in control are likely to act. We will come back to this idea later. For now, we want to draw attention to the potential instability of crime attractors because of the attention they bring. As all crimes require an offender, a high-crime place must have enough offenders, but do they need many?

The variety of proprietary places

A farmers market in a private parking lot

An apartment complex

A seafood cooperative owned by fishermen.

A single family home

A rural church and cemetery

A check cashing business

Explanation 6: Repeat Offenders

The answer is no. This is because offending concentrates. Offending patterns also look like a hockey stick: a few offenders create most of the trouble (Martinez et al., 2017). So a place may have a great deal of crime if a single prolific offender repeatedly frequents the place.

Sadly, we do not have studies tracking repeat offenders to their offending sites. If we did, we might be able to determine if most high-crime places are hot because they are frequented by a few persistent offenders. It's reasonable to assume that some high-crime places are due to repeat offending, but is this typical? Why are the repeat offenders avoiding the low-crime places? And why is no one doing something about these repeat offenders? The repeat offender explanation suggests we need to dig deeper.

Explanation 7: Inadequate Guardianship

We will now shift to three explanations that advocate for the public's role in preventing crime. The first of these focuses on people who protect targets—humans, animals, and things. Cohen and Felson (1979) called these people *guardians*. Most guardians are people engaged in their everyday routines, but some are hired for this purpose—security officers, for example. If most places are well endowed with guardianship, then crime would concentrate at the few places that are not. We cannot argue with this insight. So why are we not embracing this explanation? The answer is that it does not explain why a few places are without guardianship. We will come back to this point in explanation 9 and in the next chapter.

Some proponents of the guardianship explanation invoke Jane Jacobs' concept of "eyes on the street." This version of Jacobs' concept claims that residents and pedestrians look out for each other. Two of us (Linning & Eck, 2021) point out that this is a misreading of Jacobs. A systematic examination of Jacobs' (1961) book, *Death and Life of Great American Cities,* reveals that it is the eyes of shopkeepers—a type of place manager—that watch and who intervene. Jacobs is rather skeptical of the role of residents and strangers in keeping the peace (Linning, 2019).

Explanation 8: Poor Handling

Handlers are people who keep offenders out of trouble by threatening the removal of emotional support (Felson, 1986). Examples of potential handlers are parents, siblings, intimate partners, and sometimes clergy, teachers, close friends, and coaches. To our knowledge, no one has proposed that the distribution of handlers explains the concentration of crime across places. Still, it is theoretically possible that very low-crime places have handlers when offenders show up, but the high-crime places do not have handlers at these times. Though theoretically possible, we suspect that handling is another narrow explanation that may be important in particular circumstances but does not explain the general concentration of crime at places.

Explanation 9: Low Informal Social Control

Most guardianship and handling falls within the concept of informal social control (Wilcox et al., 2018). Many theorists contend that community functioning spontaneously creates informal social control by residents, thus suppressing crime in neighborhoods. Dysfunctional neighborhoods, often called disorganized neighborhoods, somehow fail to do this and thus have a great deal of crime. Maybe informal social control operates at places and perhaps it could explain the distribution of crime across places.

If some places have little informal social control and most places have sufficient levels, then this would create the hockey stick distribution we saw in Fig. 1.2. Indeed, Weisburd et al. (2013) have advocated that this is why proximal places—street segments—are mostly crime resistant but occasionally crime prone. They report correlations between indicators of community functioning and crime across street segments, though there is some controversy over the measures used (Braga & Clarke, 2014).

In principle the same argument could be applied to proprietary places. For apartment buildings, such an argument seems plausible. But how would it account for bars, churches, motels, parking lots, banks, and a host of other facilities without residential populations? Again, we will not throw out this idea, but we will not embrace its universality either.

Explanation 10: Bad Physical Design

The last explanation harkens back to Oscar Newman (1972), and his idea of defensible space, and to C. Ray Jeffery (1977), and his notion of crime prevention through environmental design (CPTED). Both laid great emphasis on the way the physical arrangement of space influences behavior, particularly criminal behavior. Ronald V. Clarke's (1980) theory of situational crime prevention subsumes Newman's and Jeffery's pioneering work by providing a coherent perspective (offender choice) and widening the scope to go beyond designs of buildings and large-scale structures to the designs of products and systems (Eck & Clarke, 2019).

A design explanation states that most places are designed to make them largely resistant to crime, but a few places are so poorly designed that they invite criminal predation. Examples include soundproof stairwells where victims could not call for help if attacked, stores with areas employees cannot watch, or nightclubs with multiple entrances. Newman's (1972) contrast of safe and crime-prone public housing is a good example.

In the hubristic tradition of architectural theorists, Newman asserted that design is sufficient to drive bad and good behaviors. Defensible space also takes a resident-focused approach. Newman believed that we should design buildings so that residents could identify outsiders and defend their space. Some social scientists have been skeptical (Mawby, 1977; Merry, 1981). Some evidence suggested that it was residents of the complexes, not outsiders, who were the ones committing the crimes.

The design thesis has merit, like the other explanations we have summarized. But the built environment just does not happen. Someone caused the design, caused the design alterations, or failed to cause repairs.

Too Many Explanations

There is no logical reason that the distribution of crime across places cannot arise from many loosely connected reasons. The ten explanations overlap. Two explanations deal with offenders (5 and 6), and three deal with targets and victims (2, 3, and 4). Four explanations form a cluster of explanations involving controls by noncriminal justice agents (7, 8, 9, and 10). But within a routine activity theory framework (Fig. 2.2), no single explanation will work. A crime cannot occur without some form of convergence of offenders and targets in the absence of someone who can protect the target (guardians) or deflect the offender (handlers). If there is convergence, crime at a place is likely. If convergences are common, then the place ends up in the blade of the hockey stick.

Why a place? Most crimes require offenders and their targets to be physically close to one another. A burglar must enter a building and put her hands on the stuff she wants to take. A bank robber must enter a bank and put his hands on the cash. The street robber must be within arm's length of his victim. A shoplifter must enter a store and grab the goods. An assaulter must be close enough to her target she can

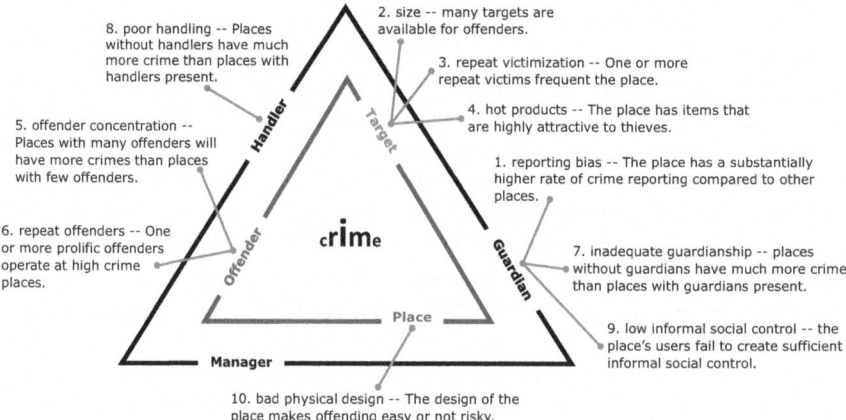

Fig. 2.2 Explanations of crime place concentration

whack or stab him. Shootings can occur within short distances, beyond arm's reach but still not too far away. There are some exceptions, such as cybercrime and mail bombing, but usually an offender has to get near his target.

Common crimes occur within distances that fit within proprietary places. Convergence is difficult if the parties involved are at opposite ends of a street segment or in different parts of a neighborhood.

We noted that the physical design explanation could not be complete because it does not address who created the design. The designs that matter must be at the place of convergence. If offenders never go to a place, any design is sufficient to thwart crime. If no targets are within a place and offenders use the place, then any design will keep them from causing trouble. Therefore, the question about who creates the design forces us to ask, who controls the place? Once we ask that question, we should also ask whether the controller of the place has influence over the factors involved in the other nine explanations. We answer these questions in the next chapter on place management.

Appendix: Three Explanations for Proximal Place Crime Concentration

What causes extreme crime levels in a few street segments rather than most? Although proximal places are not the direct concern of our book, it is worth a short digression to summarize explanations for these types of places.

Three possibilities stand out. Weisburd et al. (2013) suggest that the social disorganization thesis has been misapplied to neighborhoods: social interaction cannot occur across such large areas. Instead, social control is highly local and operates at the street segment. Their data from Seattle showed that indicators of social organization vary at the segment level, and these are correlated with crime and disorder.

A second possibility comes from Wilcox and Eck (2011). They suggest that traffic—pedestrian and vehicular—on a street segment drives crime. High trafficked segments have more businesses and more targets and draw in more offending. This idea is compatible with Weisburd, Groff, and Yang's thesis. Perhaps traffic suppresses informal social control, maybe by introducing more strangers (Tillyer & Walter, 2019).

Lee and Eck (2019) provide a third alternative. High-crime segments contain a few high-crime proprietary places on their blocks. That is, proximal place crime problems are due to proprietary place problems. Lee and Eck (2019) found that of all the high-crime street segments in Cincinnati, most had a few high-crime proprietary places (also see Lee, 2017). However, they also show that 10 percent of the high-crime street segments were crime prone their entire length. Therefore, proximal place crime problems may be due to a mix of causes—bad proprietary places, traffic volume, and inadequate social control.

Although not in the cross hairs of this book, proximal places are of interest. First, proximal places are a mix of proprietary places and streets. If proprietary place managers have influences beyond the domains of their property, it will be proximal places they influence (see Chaps. 6, 7, and 8). Second, traffic and social interactions on proximal places may enhance or mitigate place management controls on the segment. And third, proximal places are a far more plausible venue for social control than neighborhoods.

References

Andresen, M. A., & Malleson, N. (2011). Testing the stability of crime patterns: Implications for theory and policy. *Journal of Research in Crime and Delinquency, 48*(1), 58–82.

Andresen, M. A., Curman, A. S., & Linning, S. J. (2017a). The trajectories of crime at places: Understanding the patterns of disaggregated crime types. *Journal of Quantitative Criminology, 33*(3), 427–449.

Andresen, M. A., Linning, S. J., & Malleson, N. (2017b). Crime at places and spatial concentrations: Exploring the spatial stability of property crime in Vancouver BC, 2003–2013. *Journal of Quantitative Criminology, 33*(2), 255–275.

Bichler, G., Schmerler, K., & Enriquez, J. (2013). Curbing nuisance motels: An evaluation of police as place regulators. *Policing: An International Journal of Police Strategies & Management, 36*(2), 437–462.

Braga, A. A., & Clarke, R. V. (2014). Explaining high-risk concentrations of crime in the city. *Journal of Research in Crime and Delinquency, 51*(4), 480–498.

Braga, A. A., Papachristos, A. V., & Hureau, D. M. (2010). The concentration and stability of gun violence at micro places in Boston, 1980–2008. *Journal of Quantitative Criminology, 26*(1), 33–53.

Braga, A. A., Hureau, D. M., & Papachristos, A. V. (2011). The relevance of micro places to city-wide robbery trends: A longitudinal analysis of robbery incidents at street corners and block faces in Boston. *Journal of Research in Crime and Delinquency, 48*(1), 7–32.

Brantingham, P. L., & Brantingham, P. J. (1995). Criminality of place: Crime generators and crime attractors. *European Journal on Criminal Policy and Research, 3*(1), 5–26.

Buerger, M. E., Cohen, E. G., & Petrosino, A. J. (1995). Defining the "Hot Spots of Crime": Operationalizing theoretical concepts for field research. In J. E. Eck & D. Weisburd (Eds.), *Crime and place. Crime prevention studies* (Vol. 4, pp. 237–257). Criminal Justice Press.

Clarke, R. V. G. (1980). Situational' crime prevention: Theory and practice. *British Journal of Criminology, 20*(2), 136–147.

Clarke, R. V. G. (1999). *Hot products: Understanding, anticipating and reducing demand for stolen goods.* Home Office.

Clarke, R. V., & Eck, J. (2003). Become a problem-solving crime analyst: In 55 small steps. Jill Dando Institute of Crime Science, University College London.

Cohen, L. E., & Felson, M. (1979). Social change and crime rate trends: A routine activity approach. *American Sociological Review, 44*(4), 588–608.

Eck, J. E. (1994). *Drug markets and drug places: A case-control study of the spatial structure of illicit drug dealing.* Unpublished dissertation, University of Maryland, College Park.

Eck, J. E., & Clarke, R. V. G. (2019). Situational crime prevention: Theory, practice and evidence. In M. D. Krohn, N. Hendrix, G. P. Hall, & A. J. Lizotte (Eds.), *Handbook on crime and deviance* (pp. 355–376). Springer International Publishing.

References

Eck, J. E., Lee, Y., O, S., & Martinez, N. N. (2017). Compared to what? Estimating the relative concentration of crime at places using systematic and other reviews. *Crime Science, 6*(1), 2–17. https://doi.org/10.1186/s40163-017-0070-4

Farrell, G. (2015). Crime concentration theory. *Crime Prevention and Community Safety, 17*(4), 233–248.

Farrell, G., & Sousa, W. (1998). Repeat victimization and hot spots: The overlap and its implications for crime control and problem-oriented policing. In R. V. G. Clarke (Ed.), *Crime prevention studies* (pp. 221–240). Criminal Justice Press.

Felson, M. (1986). Linking criminal choices, routine activities, informal control, and criminal outcomes. In D. B. Cornish & R. V. Clarke (Eds.), *The reasoning criminal: Rational choice perspectives on offending* (pp. 119–128). Springer-Verlag.

Felson, M. (2016). The routine activities approach. In R. Wortley & M. Townsley (Eds.), *Environmental criminology and crime analysis* (2nd ed., pp. 87–97). Routledge.

Groff, E. R., Weisburd, D., & Yang, S.-M. (2010). Is it important to examine crime trends at a local 'micro' level?: A longitudinal analysis of street to street variability in crime trajectories. *Journal of Quantitative Criminology, 26*(1), 7–32.

Grove, L. E., Farrell, G., Farrington, D. P., & Johnson, S. (2012). *Preventing repeat victimization: A systematic review.* Brå - The Swedish National Council for Crime Prevention.

Jacobs, J. (1961). *The death and life of great American cities.* Vintage.

Jeffery, C. R. (1977). *Crime prevention through environmental design.* Sage.

Lee, Y. (2017). *Comparing measures of the concentration of crime at places and times.* Unpublished dissertation, University of Cincinnati, Cincinnati.

Lee, Y., & Eck, J. E. (2019). Comparing measures of the concentration of crime at places. *Crime Prevention and Community Safety, 21*(4), 269–294.

Linning, S. J. (2019). *The neo-Jacobian perspective of place and neighborhood crime: A case study of property ownership, redevelopment, and crime in Walnut Hills, Cincinnati, Ohio.* Unpublished dissertation, University of Cincinnati, Cincinnati.

Linning, S. J., & Eck, J. E. (2021). *Whose "eyes on the street" control crime? Expanding place management into neighborhoods.* Cambridge University Press.

Martinez, N. N., Lee, Y., Eck, J. E., & O, S.-H. (2017). Ravenous wolves revisited: A systematic review of offending concentration. *Crime Science, 6*(1), 10. https://doi.org/10.1186/s40163-017-0072-2

Matthews, R., Pease, C., & Pease, K. (2001). Repeated bank robbery: Theme and variations. In G. Farrell & K. Pease (Eds.), *Repeat victimization* (pp. 133–151). Criminal Justice Press.

Mawby, R. I. (1977). Defensible space: A theoretical and empirical appraisal. *Urban Studies, 14,* 169–179.

Merry, S. E. (1981). Defensible space undefended: Social factors in crime control through environmental design. *Urban Affairs Review, 16*(4), 397–422.

Newman, O. (1972). *Defensible space: Crime prevention through urban design.* Macmillan.

O, S.-H., Martinez, N. N., Lee, Y., & Eck, J. E. (2017). How concentrated is crime among victims? A systematic review from 1970 to 2014. *Crime Science, 6*(6). https://doi.org/10.1186/s40163-017-0069-x

Payne, T. C., & Gallagher, K. (2016). The importance of small units of aggregation: Trajectories of crime at addresses in Cincinnati, Ohio, 1998–2012. *Criminology, Criminal Justice Law, and Society, 17*(1), 20–36.

Polvi, N., Looman, T., Humphries, C., & Pease, K. (1991). The time course of repeat burglary victimization. *British Journal of Criminology, 31*(4), 411–414.

Sherman, L. W., Gartin, P. R., & Buerger, M. E. (1989). Hot spots of predatory crime: Routine activities and the criminology of place. *Criminology, 27*(1), 27–55.

Sidebottom, A., & Bowers, K. (2010). Bag theft in bars: An analysis of relative risk, perceived risk and modus operandi. *Security Journal, 23*(3), 206–224.

Spelman, W. (1995). Criminal careers of public places. In J. E. Eck & D. Weisburd (Eds.), *Crime and place* (pp. 115–144). Criminal Justice Press.

Steenbeek, W., & Weisburd, D. (2016). Where the action is in crime? An examination of variability of crime across different spatial units in The Hague, 2001–2009. *Journal of Quantitative Criminology, 32*(3), 449–469.

Tillyer, M. S., & Walter, R. J. (2019). Busy businesses and busy contexts: The distribution and sources of crime at commercial properties. *Journal of Research in Crime and Delinquency, 56*(6), 816–850.

Walter, R. J., Tillyer, M. S., & Acolin, A. (2022). Spatiotemporal crime patterns across six U.S. cities: Analyzing stability and change in clusters and outliers. *Journal of Quantitative Criminology.* https://doi.org/10.1007/s10940-022-09556-7

Wartell, J., Zidar, M., & Bridges, K. (2021). *Crime science and Boulder Crime.* Presentation to city council, June 22. Boulder: Boulder Police Department. https://boulder.novusagenda.com/agendapublic/VODPreview.aspx?meetingVideoID=82b1934e-7cad-4bcf-82ae-14614a51c4c6&index=5

Weisburd, D., Bushway, S., Lum, C., & Yang, S.-M. (2004). Crime trajectories at places: A longitudinal study of street segments in the city of Seattle. *Criminology, 42*(2), 283–322.

Weisburd, D., Morris, N. A., & Groff, E. R. (2009). Hot spots of juvenile crime: A longitudinal study of arrest incidents at street segments in Seattle, Washington. *Journal of Quantitative Criminology, 25*(4), 443–467.

Weisburd, D., Groff, E. R., & Yang, S.-M. (2013). *The criminology of place: Street segments and our understanding of the crime problem.* Oxford University Press.

Wenger, M. R., & Lantz, B. (2022). Hate crime and place: The spatial and temporal concentration of bias-motivated crime in Washington, D.C. *Journal of Interpersonal Violence, 37*(13–14), NP10683–708.

Wilcox, P., & Eck, J. E. (2011). Criminology of the unpopular. *Criminology & Public Policy, 10*(2), 473–482.

Wilcox, P., Cullen, F. T., & Feldmeyer, B. (2018). *Communities and crime: An enduring American challenge.* Temple University Press.

Chapter 3
Place Management

The ten explanations in the last chapter are pieces of a larger explanation. In this chapter, we give that explanation. We show why place management provides a unifying answer. We begin by defining *place managers*, the people who operate proprietary places. We then describe what they do, the four functions of place management. Then we demonstrate how place management unifies the ten explanations we discussed in the previous chapter. Before concluding the chapter, we examine specific actions place managers can take to fight crime and the evidence showing these actions work.

Place Managers

In Chap. 1 we described place managers as anyone who has authority to operate a place. Here we provide more details. They gain their authority by owning the property—all homeowners are place managers, for example—or by being the recipient of the owner's delegated authority (more in Chap. 4). A store clerk is a place manager because the owner gave him authority over some aspects of the business at the place. The business owner is a place manager by owning the business. If she rents space for her business, her rental or lease agreement conveys some of the property owner's authority to her. A volunteer in a pet rescue clinic is a place manager if the clinic's director gave him authority.

Customers are not place managers, usually. However, in special circumstances, the operator of the place may authorized a place user to act as a place manager. For example, John and his wife often breakfast at a rural diner. When the cook is busy, regular customers go behind the counter, pick up the coffee pot, and pour coffee for all the other customers. On occasion, a customer will brew the coffee. We will treat such arrangements as rare.

Although the concept of a place manager is simple, in practice the limits of the role can be other than simple. Two of us rent units in high-rise condominiums. As renters, our place management authority comes through our leases with the owners of our condominium units. For the most part, our place management authority is restricted to the unit, although our leases provide rights to other areas (e.g., parking spaces). Our landlords are place managers with wider authority. The width of their authority depends on the details of their property deeds and their condominium association's by-laws. The condominium association manages common areas (halls, entry foyer, laundry facility, exercise space, grounds around the building, and so on) but not the insides of the units. Further complicating the arrangements are the condominium associations' service contracts—for common area cleaning, security, grounds keeping, and other services—with property management companies. These companies and their employees are place managers, too. Who is not a place manager? Visitors, package delivery drivers, repair crews, moving company employees, healthcare workers attending residents, and many others.

A place manager can have many roles. Consider a mother who owns a house. She is a place manager for that house. She is a handler of her teen son and daughter. She is a guardian of the family's belongings and her children. A store clerk, as we noted, is a place manager. In this role, he may have guardianship responsibilities for the goods and fixtures in the store and for his customers.

All places have place managers. For public parks, the city's parks department is the place manager. Public works departments are the place managers of city sidewalks. Even vacant buildings have place managers. Someone's name is on the property deed for the building. Therefore, when crime is a problem at a vacant place, it is not because of the absence of a place manager. It is because the place manager chooses not to act.

In the next section, we describe how a place manager influences crime. Before we do, we must head off a common confusion. Place managers do not operate like guardians. Danielle Reynald (2009) posits three layers of guardianship. A guardian must be present. The guardian must watch. And a guardian must be willing to intervene. These are not requirements of place management. A place manager can be absent, not watching, and not intervening and still thwart crime. How this can be? We will see when we look at place management functions.

The Four Functions of Place Management

Tamara was the first to describe what place managers do (Madensen, 2007). She assigned them four functions, whose first letters spell the acronym ORCA. Place managers organize space. They regulate conduct. They control access. And they acquire resources.

None of these functions are explicitly about crime. Although guardianship and handling are defined relative to their roles in crime control, place management is not. Most place management activities are not about crime, at least directly. Place management is operating the place: be it a home, business, government agency, or not-for-profit organization. Although not directly about crime, each of the four functions has profound impacts on crime.

Each function encourages some behaviors and discourages other behaviors. Criminologists dwell on processes that limit unwanted behavior. But encouragement is important to place management. Sometimes, place managers must make choices between the actions they want to encourage (e.g., shopping) and those they want to discourage (e.g., theft).

Organization of Space

This first function encompasses all physical features of a place: deciding to operate at a specific location; arranging walls, windows, and doors to divide the place; choosing wall colors and other decorations; selecting of background sound; and many more actions. The placement of curb cuts connecting the parking area to the street is part of this function, as well as all outside landscaping and signage. The decision of where to locate the bar relative to the dance floor in a club or how to configure aisles in a convenience store falls under this function too. The maintenance of the physical aspects of the place is also part of this function. These choices may have implications for crime, but place managers often chose them with other things in mind.

Nevertheless, crime does drive some physical design choices. Most defensible space, crime prevention through environmental design, and situational crime prevention activities influence the organization of space. Because only a place manager has the authority to alter the space, these crime prevention tactics are all place management acts.

Place management

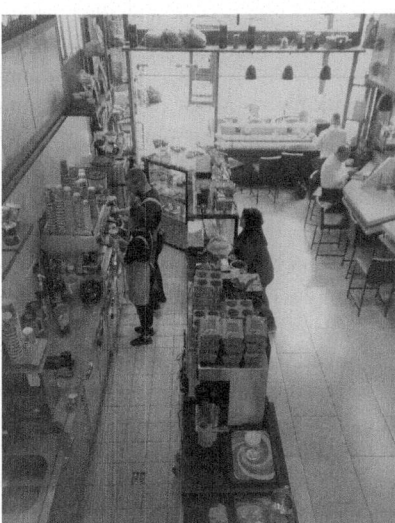

The organization of space in a London coffee shop. The signs (below) illustrate access control and regulation of conduct.

Regulation of Conduct

Place managers want place users to behave in particular ways. A store owner wants people to buy things. A restaurant owner wants customers to eat. The leader of a place of worship wants members to gain spiritual uplift. The head of an outpatient drug rehabilitation center wants clients to shake their addiction. Therefore, the place managers of each of these places will try to encourage activities that lead to these outcomes.

There are behaviors that the place manager wants to discourage. Some of these are crimes but most are merely undesirable. The shopkeeper probably prefers people to shop rather than hang out and write a novel. The librarian probably does not want loud singing or cheering: activities that might be embraced by the karaoke bar owner down the street or by the sports stadium manager several blocks away.

Place managers use many techniques to regulate behavior. Some are overt: signage encouraging or discouraging behaviors, for example. Movie theaters use videos to tell patrons to silence their cell phones before the main feature. On airplanes, flight attendants give the rules, and written rules are put in the seat pocket. Other techniques are subtle or rely on social convention. If a coffee shop owner wants customers to buy more food and drinks, they offer free Wi-Fi to encourage patrons to spend more time there. If a place manager wants customers to line up, they may organize the space to encourage a queue.

Control of Access

Just as place managers want some activities but not others, they want some place users but not others. In our homes, we want our friends to visit, but only during specific times. Office buildings want employees and those doing business with employees. The building owner may employ a concierge to assist desired visitors and discourage undesired place users. Advertising by place managers helps place users to self-select: an advertisement for a cowboy theme bar displaying the logo of a mass-produced beer-like substance will keep out most craft beer enthusiasts. Ticket sales screen in patrons and screen out others. Even curb cuts encourage and discourage through their placement along busy streets. Opening hours drive access control routines.

Although place managers use access control for a variety of purposes, some have a crime control function. That is why when the place is not in active use, the manager locks the doors. Bar patrons who routinely drink too much and create disturbances get banned. Apartment owners sometimes exchange information about prospective tenants to avoid renting to problem people. They also give key fobs for entry into the building to tenants who have signed leases. A shelter for women may ban men from entering to avoid disturbances and assaults.

Acquisition of Resources

All proprietary places need resources to operate. Resources are tied to successful operation of the place either directly or indirectly. Businesses get their income from operations at the place. Nongovernmental organizations may have to demonstrate to donors that the place is functioning as planned (e.g., a soup kitchen may have to show how many people it served). And government agencies operating places must get budget allocations from elected representatives. For businesses, resource acquisition may be the purpose for existing. Owner-occupied homes require the place manager to have an income from another source.

Resource availability drives the other three ORCA functions. Without sufficient resources, place managers will have difficulty changing or maintaining the organization of space. Without resources, place managers may find it hard to regulate conduct. And without resources, they may have trouble controlling access.

Resources aid place management, but they can also attract offenders. Stores stock goods to make sales, but the goods are desired by shoplifters. Cash in the till is a tempting target for thieves. Like the other place management functions, acquisition of resources can discourage and encourage crime.

By now it should be apparent that these functions intertwine. Organization of space must be coordinated with regulation of conduct and control of access to be effective. The nightclub bouncer is an emblem of access control, but the door behind him is pure space organization. The bouncer without the door or the door without the bouncer is less effective. If the same bouncer instructs eager patrons on how to behave in line and after entry, he is regulating conduct. If he screens people based on their expected spending activity, he is influencing resource acquisition.

The function of the place drives how the place manager implements the four ORCA functions. ORCA touches decisions about hiring, training, scheduling, supervision, and planning. Crime is usually an impediment to the business of the place, so some ORCA activities may be explicitly directed toward thwarting crime. But place managers undertake many, if not most, ORCA activities to accomplish positive ends: having a good night's sleep, selling things, entertaining, improving people's health, and so on. Even a place used by a criminal justice agency may have higher priorities than crime control.

Place Management as a Keystone Explanation

Place management influences all ten explanations we discussed in the previous chapter. The schematic in Fig. 3.1 illustrates this point. Each ORCA function (left column) creates two or more of the explanations (center column). The third column shows which routine activity element is implicated the most. Place management, therefore, can trigger many crime prevention mechanisms simultaneously. Let's look at each ORCA function separately.

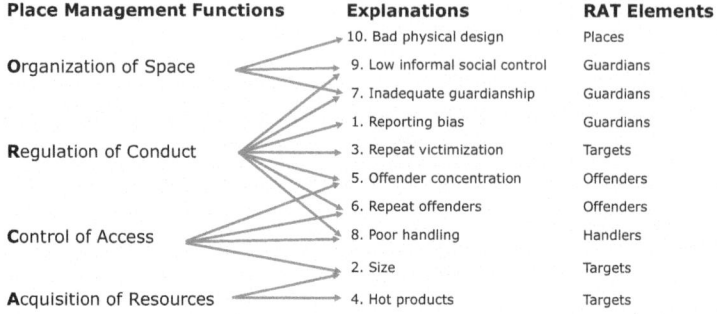

Fig. 3.1 Place management and explanations of place crime concentration. (See Eck and Madensen (2018))

Organization of Space

This function helps explain physical design, not surprisingly. But it also influences informal social control and guardianship. The ability of people to watch out for each other depends in part on sightlines and lighting. Walls, displays of goods, and other barriers can interrupt sightlines and make it hard for people to look out for each other. Guardianship, perhaps the most meaningful aspect of informal social control, will be inhibited by such barriers. Poor lighting has much the same effect. So this place management function is important for guardianship and places.

Regulation of Conduct

The second function has the most influence, measured in connections to many explanations. Conduct regulation can encourage informal social control by helping place users build connections. This is probably most useful when many place users are repeat users. One of our students wrote a term paper about a gun store; the owner invited his friends to hang out so there would always be an organized community available to deter robberies. Place managers can create guardianship in several ways. Most obviously, they can hire security officers, loss prevention agents, bouncers, concierges, and other designated guardians. Place managers also can build guardianship into the duties of employees by training and supervising them. A third way is to explicitly foster guardianship among place users. Airport announcements asking flyers to report suspicious bags is an obvious example. Recruiting place users will influence crime reporting rates.

Regulation can also influence repeat victimization and offenders. Place managers can encourage others to engage in behaviors that protect vulnerable place users or restrict behaviors that make people more vulnerable (e.g., overdrinking at bars). If offenders are provoked by others' behavior, then regulating the provoking behaviors may reduce offenders. Banning known offenders may also reduce crime, particularly if those banned are chronic offenders. Encouraging handling may help, particularly if the offenders are young. Some shopping centers and malls restrict access by juveniles by requiring them to be accompanied by a parent (Rawe, 2007).

Control of Access

As the previous example demonstrates, access control overlaps with conduct regulation. Place managers often combine access control with signs explaining rules and procedures (regulation of conduct). One way bars and pubs control violence is by banning patrons who get into fights. Landlords may refuse to rent to people known to violate lease conditions. Stores sometimes exclude known shoplifters. The authors have observed stores that restrict the number of young people who can enter at one time. Even owners of single-family homes stop inviting guests who are nuisances. Place managers may also restrict people at high risk of victimization. Children, for example, are excluded from some locations for this reason. Parking restrictions can keep vehicles out of places where theft is common. A place manager may put high-theft items in a special room and require customers to ask an employee to see them.

Acquisition of Resources

Not stocking items at high risk of theft illustrates the point that crime prevention and resource acquisition sometimes work at cross purposes. Mass retailers rely on many customers and a wide variety of items, thus increasing crime target density. In essence, their business plan creates a crime generator. They may treat the consequential theft as a cost of doing business (Zidar et al., 2018). To gain resources, some place managers choose to stock hot products. Unless other prevention measures are taken, this will result in high-crime levels.

Crime Prevention Within Places

Situational Crime Prevention

What prevention measures can place managers take? Ronald V. Clarke answered this question in a series of scientific papers, theoretical articles, and practical guides (Clarke 1980, 1995; Clarke & Eck, 2009). His answer is situational crime prevention. Situational crime prevention begins with the commonsense idea that people make most decisions intuitively. They take in signs from the physical and social characteristics of their immediate settings. Settings are usually places. Place characteristics signal would be offenders whether crime is a good idea or not.

Clarke lists five signals answering offender relevant questions. Will I need a great deal of effort to succeed at this crime? Do I face too high a risk of being caught? Are my rewards of crime too low? Are there too few provocations for acting badly? Do I have few excuses for committing crimes? If the answers to these questions are mostly "Yes," then crime is not tempting. If the place signals "No" to most of these questions, then crime is tempting and is a likely choice. The few high-crime places in the blade of the hockey stick present chronic temptations to would-be offenders.

What can place managers do to make their locations less tempting to possible offenders? (Clarke, 1980, 1995; Eck & Clarke, 2019) suggests five techniques for each of the five signals. We list these 25 techniques in Table 3.1. For each, we give an example from a retail store setting. If we had chosen owner-occupied homes, churches, taverns, or hair solons, we would have used different examples. Few places apply all the techniques: some are inappropriate, some too expensive, and others conflict with place functioning. However, almost all safe places will use some of these techniques. And all techniques work at some place, even if rarely applied.

Only place managers can implement these techniques. If the police or others want to drive down crime at a place, they must enlist the support of the place manager. Only items 14 (disrupting markets), 20 (discouraging imitation), and 25 (controlling drugs and alcohol) would be substantially improved by the assistance of police or others who have no control over the place.

Evidence Situational Prevention Works at Places

Do these techniques work? Can place managers suppress crime? Since Clarke first described situational crime prevention, there have been many evaluations of its application at places. Three systematic reviews of these evaluations demonstrate that situational crime prevention can be effective (Eck, 2002; Guerette, 2009; Eck & Guerette, 2012).

In the most recent review, the authors examined 149 evaluations of situational prevention at residential, retail, transportation, recreation, and public places. In these evaluations, authors examined a variety of crimes including property, violent, disorder, and drug offenses. For the 39 residential evaluations (mostly apartment buildings), 77 percent showed evidence of effectiveness. For the 25 retail evaluations (various shops and stores), 88 percent suppressed crime. For the 26 transportation evaluations (buses, trains, ferries, and so forth), 88 percent were effective. Of all seven recreational places (all drinking places), all prevented crime. And for the 52 public places (usually streets, alleys, and sidewalks), 62 percent were successful.

Conclusions

Table 3.1 Situational crime prevention techniques with examples from retail stores

Increase effort	Increase risk	Reduce rewards	Reduce provocations	Reduce excuses
1. *Harden targets:* securing electronic products with cables	6. *Extend guardianship:* ask shoppers to watch for shoplifters	11. *Conceal targets:* place surplus stock out of customers' sight	16. *Reduce frustration:* keep lines short, provide help	21. *Set rules:* have clear product return policies
2. *Control access:* limit entry portals and opening times	7. *Assist natural surveillance:* provide good lighting, remove blind spots	12. *Remove targets:* do not stock high-theft items	17. *Avoid disputes:* clarify procedures; put price tags on items	22. *Post instructions:* use signs to explain processes
3. *Screen exits:* use electronic alarm tags on products	8. *Reduce anonymity:* have employees greet shoppers on entry	13. *Identify property:* mark items with store logo	18. *Reduce arousal:* create a friendly calm environment	23. Alert conscience: post signs saying, "Shoplifting hurts all of us"
4. *Deflect offenders:* require juveniles to be accompanied by an adult	9. *Use place managers:* have employees assist customers	14. *Disrupt markets:* identify and report stores that resell stolen goods	19. *Neutralize peer pressure:* limit size of juvenile groups allowed in store	24. *Assist compliance:* make paying for products easy and quick
5. *Control tools:* prohibit backpacks and tote bags in store	10. *Strengthen surveillance:* use obvious CCTV	15. *Deny benefits:* use ink tags	20. *Discourage imitation:* make theft invisible to store patrons	25. *Control drugs and alcohol:* prohibit drinking in store

Adapted from Clarke and Eck (2009), Eck and Clarke (2019)

Across all the places, place managers' application of situational crime prevention was helpful in 77 percent of the evaluations.

Conclusions

Our tour of the links between place management and explanations of crime demonstrates the range of controls place managers can exercise over crime. It also shows that their controls have layers: regulation of conduct often overlaps with organization of space and control of access. As the third column in Fig. 3.1 shows, place managers reach all elements of routine activity theory. This does not mean they have total control over place crime. It does mean that they have considerable control and considerable flexibility in how they exercise this control. The evidence from evaluations of situational crime prevention shows that place management control of crime is real: it is not just a conjecture.

What gives place managers the power to exercise control? The answer is obvious. They own the place or have authority provided by the owner. This answer is fine, as far as it goes. But we need to look at the sources of powers in greater detail. That is the subject of the next chapter.

References

Clarke, R. V. G., & Eck, J. E. (2009). *Crime analysis for problem solvers: In 60 small steps*. Office of Community Policing Services.

Clarke, R. V. G. (1980). Situational crime prevention: Theory and practice. *British Journal of Criminology, 20*(2), 136–47.

Clarke, R. V. G. (1995). Situational crime prevention. In M. Tonry & D. P. Farrington (Eds.), *Building a safer society: Strategic approaches to crime prevention* (pp. 91–150). University of Chicago Press.

Eck, J. E. (2002). Preventing crime at places. In L. W. Sherman, D. Farrington, B. Welsh, & D. L. MacKenzie (Eds.), *Evidence-based crime prevention* (pp. 241–294). Routledge.

Eck, J. E., & Clarke, R. V. G. (2019). Situational crime prevention: Theory, practice and evidence. In M. D. Krohn, N. Hendrix, G. P. Hall, & A. J. Lizotte (Eds.), *Handbook on crime and deviance* (pp. 355–376). Springer International Publishing.

Eck, J. E., & Guerette, R. T. (2012). Place-based crime prevention: Theory, evidence, and policy. In D. P. Farrington & B. C. Welsh (Eds.), *The Oxford handbook of crime prevention* (pp. 354–383). Oxford University Press.

Eck, J. E., & Madensen, T. D. (2018). Place management, guardianship, and the establishment of order. In D. S. Nagin, F. T. Cullen, & C. L. Jonson (Eds.), *Deterrence, choice, and crime: Contemporary perspectives* (pp. 269–296). Routledge.

Guerette, R. T. (2009). The push, pull, and expansion of situational crime prevention evaluation: An appraisal of thirty-seven years of research. In J. Knutsson & N. Tilley (Eds.), *Evaluating crime reduction initiatives* (pp. 29–58). Criminal Justice Press.

Madensen, T. D. (2007). *Bar management and crime: Toward a dynamic theory of place management and crime hotspots*. Unpublished doctoral dissertation, University of Cincinnati, Cincinnati.

Rawe, J. (2007). Bye-bye, mall rats. *Time*. June 28. http://content.time.com/time/magazine/article/0,9171,1638449,00.html. Accessed 12 Aug 2022.

Reynald, D. M. (2009). Guardianship in action: Developing a new tool for measurement. *Crime Prevention and Community Safety: An International Journal, 11*(1), 1–20.

Zidar, M. S., Shafer, J. G., & Eck, J. E. (2018). Reframing an obvious police problem: Discovery, analysis and response to a manufactured problem in a small city. *Policing: A Journal of Policy and Practice, 12*(3), 316–331.

Chapter 4
Sources of Powers

Being Explicit About Sources of Control Powers

If an institution can control crime, it must have a source of power. The source is obvious for formal control; it is the state. The government has the authority to back its demands with force. It is more difficult to pin down the source of power for informal social control. In part, this is because informal social control is a grab bag of non-state controls (Greenberg & Rohe, 1984). It is any social control that is not police control. But even this distinction is fuzzy as we will show later. Is place management a type of informal social control? Like neighborhood residents, place managers are not state actors. Like residents, they are in communities. Like informal social control actors, they employ guardianship.

Despite these similarities this chapter argues that place management is a very different type of control. The biggest difference is its source of authority to exert control. We start by describing the elements of a good definition of control. Then we examine researchers' definitions of informal social control in light of these elements. We then return to place managers and explain the source of their authority to govern what goes on at their places. In contrast to informal social control, place management powers are considerable and grounded in law.

Defining Forms of Control

A definition of a control mechanism must contain five elements. It must specify who is controlling. It must describe the actions controllers take. It must stipulate the subjects of their control. It must indicate the purposes for controlling these subjects. And it must identify the sources of power backing the control. We can organize these five elements as a formula.

$$X \text{ does } A \text{ to } T \text{ to achieve } G, \text{ using } P. \tag{4.1}$$

In formula (4.1), X are the people exerting control, A are their actions, T are the people who the Xs are trying to control, G are the goals Xs want to achieve with their actions, and P are the powers Xs require to take the actions (A). If a definition cannot provide sufficient information to describe these five elements, the definition is vague.

Formula (4.1) is a template for a sentence in the active voice. Using information from the previous chapter, we can fill in the formula to define place management:

$$(X) \text{Property owners, and their delegates,} (A) \text{apply ORCA functions on their property to guide} (T) \text{place users} (G) \text{to achieve place-specific goals,} (P) \text{using} \underline{\qquad}. \tag{4.2}$$

Like all sentences, it contains words that other sentences define. From the previous chapter, *delegates* means people to whom the place owner has conferred authority, such as employees, renters, and contractors. We also described the four ORCA functions earlier. Place users vary by place: family members in a residential house, drinkers in a bar, worshipers in a church, inmates in a jail, and so forth. Similarly, the goals of place managers vary by place. We have left the last clause of the sentence blank. We will fill it in at the end of the chapter.

Let's turn now to informal social control.

What Is Community Informal Social Control?

The concept of informal social control is so widely used that many researchers do not bother to define it when discussing the concept (Linning et al., 2022). This is unfortunate because those who define it give different definitions. We reviewed definitions given by prominent researchers in several prominent articles to determine the consistency of their definitions and whether we can complete formula (4.1) with the information they give.

X: Actors

Several researchers gave very broad descriptions such as citizens, adults, or public (Carr, 2003, p. 1249; Groff, 2015, p. 90; Nash & Bowen, 1999, p. 173; Sargeant et al., 2021, p. 3). Some studies include police as actors (Schulenberg, 2016, p. 461), while others explicitly rule out police (Greenberg & Rohe, 1984, p. 48). More frequently, researchers specified neighbors or residents (Burchfield, 2009, pp. 46–7; Greenberg & Rohe, 1984, p. 48; Kubrin & Weitzer, 2003, pp. 375–6; Sampson et al., 1997, p. 918; Silver & Miller, 2004, p. 553; Warner, 2014, p. 421; Wickes et al., 2017, p. 102). We will assume that informal control is exerted by people who live in an area, although there is some disagreement.

A: Actions

Many researchers do not describe the acts taken to exert control (Carr, 2003, p. 1249; Groff, 2015, p. 90; Silver & Miller, 2004, p. 553; Warner, 2014, p. 421). Others used watching or a synonym (surveilling, monitoring). These same researchers also described actions such as questioning, intervening, confronting, admonishing, or scolding (Burchfield, 2009, pp. 46–7; Greenberg & Rohe, 1984, p. 48; Kubrin & Weitzer, 2003, pp. 375–6; Nash & Bowen, 1999, p. 173; Sampson et al., 1997, p. 918; Wickes et al., 2017, p. 102; Sargeant et al., 2021, p. 3). There was an assortment of other actions described: gossip, disapproval, talking, and working together (Kubrin & Weitzer, 2003, p. 375–6; Sampson et al., 1997, p. 918; Wickes et al., 2017, p. 102). A few definitions explicitly mentioned calling the police (Sargeant et al., 2021, p. 3; Wickes et al., 2017, p. 102). Wickes and colleagues (2017, p. 102) added involving other government agencies. It is difficult to determine if calling the police is widely accepted among researchers as a form of informal social control. Because two of Danielle Reynald's (2009) criteria for guardianship are repeatedly mentioned—watching and intervening—we will summarize informal social control actions using *guardianship*, even though some authors are more expansive.

T: Targets

Who do researchers list as targets of informal control? Many do not give a specific answer (Burchfield, 2009, pp. 46–7; Carr, 2003, p. 1249; Groff, 2015, p. 90; Sargeant et al., 2021, p. 3; Warner, 2014, p. 421). But when researchers mention a target, it is inevitably children, youth, or teenagers (Greenberg & Rohe, 1984, p. 48; Kubrin & Weitzer, 2003, pp. 375–6; Nash & Bowen, 1999, p. 173; Sampson et al., 1997, p. 918; Silver & Miller, 2004, p. 553; Wickes et al., 2017, p. 102). Only Greenberg and Rohe (1984, p. 48) explicitly suggest strangers. Sampson and partners (1997, p. 918) nominated persons and adults. It is safe to say that youth are the consensus target of informal social control, although there are a range of opinions.

G: Goals

One would expect the purpose of informal control to be clear. This might explain why some researchers did not give a reason (Greenberg & Rohe, 1984, p. 48; Kubrin & Weitzer, 2003, p. 375–6; Wickes et al., 2017, p. 102). When papers provided a goal for exerting informal social control, they were most likely to say prevention of crime and disorder (Carr, 2003, p.1249; Sampson et al., 1997, p. 918; Silver & Miller, 2004, p. 553; Warner, 2014, p. 421). Others gave ambiguous goals consistent with the idea of disorder: reduce truancy, hanging out, and unacceptable behavior or uphold order, codes, norms, and acceptable conduct (Groff, 2015, p. 90; Nash & Bowen, 1999, p. 173; Sargeant et al., 2021, p. 3). Burchfield (2009, pp. 46–7) mysteriously suggested the goal is "the community good." Ignoring the researchers who gave no goals or gave hopelessly general goals, we interpret the goal of informal social control as keeping crime and disorder down.

P: Powers

We could find no study that explains where residents get their authority to exert control over young people or over anyone else. Perhaps researchers assume that residents will mobilize formal authority, police. Or that adult residents possess moral powers—e.g., ostracism—that inhibit youth misbehavior. Or that youth crave adult approval and quail at the prospect of adult disapproval.

We have looked at what leading scholars say about each of the five elements for a coherent definition of informal social control. There is considerable ambiguity and variation, which we ignore. We will focus on our interpretation of the modal responses of researchers. We will not guess at the power source. This yields a statement like the following. Informal social control is:

$$(X) \text{Community residents} (A) \text{exerting guardianship over} (T) \text{community youth} (G) \text{to prevent crime and disorder,} (P) \text{using} \underline{\qquad}. \quad (4.3)$$

Formula (4.3) is very different than formula (4.2), so we should not confuse informal social control with place management.

If formula (4.3) describes informal social control, then can informal social control suppress burglary, drug dealing, robbery, car theft, and assault? Many studies report negative correlations between informal social control and these crimes. Almost all of these studies measure crime and control at the same time—so they cannot tell which came first control or crime. Perhaps high crime rates reduce controls. Rebecca Wickes and John R. Hipp (2018) collected data that allowed them to tell which came first. They found little reason to believe informal social control reduces crime. Informal social control may be too weak (see also, Wickes et al., 2017).

The Source of Power of Place Managers

Our excursion into informal social control had two objectives. The first was to pin down this concept to show that it does not embrace place management. We know this for two reasons. First, the researchers we reviewed made no explicit reference to people who own and operate property. Second, place managers may not live in the neighborhood. Some do live in the area where their place is located. Occupiers of their own single-family detached houses are the prime example of this. So are condominium owners. But many place managers live elsewhere: landlords of apartment complexes, owners of small and large businesses, government employees, and many others. What qualifies a person as a place manager is that they own property or receive authority from someone who owns it (something we return to shortly). They can live anywhere.

Our second reason for examining informal social control was to draw attention to sources of power. This topic is underdeveloped among informal social control researchers. That is not the case with place management. The source of power of place management is ownership. Ownership conveys property rights and obligations on others.

Property Rights

There are many reasons people prefer to buy a home rather than rent. Ownership allows them to transform the building as they desire; to allow guests to stay for as long as they wish; to undertake repairs of broken fixtures; to set the rules of behavior; not to be worried that the property owner will refuse to renew their lease; and to build wealth.

Ownership conveys property rights in a place. But the meaning of *ownership* is complex:

> In common speech, we frequently speak of someone owning this land, that house, or these bonds. This conversational style ... masks the variety and complexity of the ownership relationship. What is owned are rights to use resources, including one's body and mind, and these rights are always circumscribed, often by the prohibition of certain actions. To "own land" usually means to have the right to till (or not to till) the soil, to mine the soil, to offer those rights for sale, etc., but not to have the right to throw soil at a passerby, to use it to change the course of a stream, or to force someone to buy it. What are owned are socially recognized rights of action. (Alchian & Demsetz, 1973, p. 17)

The use of the plural *rights* in this quote is instructive. When you purchase a building and its lot, you are purchasing multiple rights. The rights you purchase helps determine the price you will pay. Imagine two large lots, identical in all respects, except one has a deed restriction prohibiting building on the rear acreage to conserve a wetland. Both properties are for sale. In all likelihood, the property without the conservation easement will sell for more than the property with it. That is because the owner's right to use the rear acreage is unencumbered in one instance and limited in the other.

Among scholars of property rights and law, the dominant metaphor for the multiplicity of rights is a bundle of sticks: each stick representing a right (Merrill & Smith, 2010):

More than one party can claim some ownership interest in the same resource. One party may own the right to till the land, while another, perhaps the state, may own an easement to traverse or otherwise use the land for specific purposes. It is not the resource itself which is owned; it is a bundle, or a portion, of rights to use a resource that is owned (Alchian & Demsetz, 1973, p. 17).

Property rights

An order of monks owned and operated this monastery. They were the place managers until, in 1539, King Henry VIII of England seized the property. He then sold the property, transferring the property rights.

Today, a historic preservation organization owns and operates this World Heritage Site. It organizes the space, regulates conduct, controls access, and acquires resources.

Rights That May Be Included in a Bundle of Rights

There are many possible sticks in these bundles. One reason is that there are many forms of property and people's interests in these forms vary widely. Our interest is in *real property*, usually land and buildings. We will describe eight rights, drawing upon the classic article by British legal scholar, Anthony M. Honore' (1961), Denise R. Johnson's (2015) discussion of property rights, Edella Schlaeger and Elinor Ostrom's (1992) well cited piece, and rights highlighted in the training of real estate brokers (Kenton, 2020). Because different scholars give different names to the same rights and some scholars group several rights under a single term that other scholars enumerate separately, we chose names for each right that may differ from the names used in the cited sources.

Alteration: The right to alter the property People who own property can usually alter it as they see fit. Schlaeger and Ostrom (1992) combine this right with several others under the term "manage," and Kenton (2020) calls this right *control*.

This right allows property owners to organize space without the interference of nonowners. It also implies a duty on nonowners to refrain from altering the property without permission. This is why all crime prevention strategies that suggest changing physical design—defensible space, crime prevention through environmental design, and situational crime prevention—must be implemented with the consent of the owner or after gaining a court order.

Like all rights, it is not absolute; zoning, health and safety legislation, homeowner association regulations, and other rules may restrict these rights. Despite these limitations, the right to alter the property allows a wide variety of space reconfiguration and choices of decorations.

Control: The right to limit what people on the property can do This is the right that facilitates regulation of conduct. We use Kenton's (2020) term, control even though some commentators tie this right to other sticks and call it *manage* (Honore', 1961; Johnson, 2015; Schlaeger & Ostrom, 1992). A homeowner can set rules of decorum for her house. A library can establish rules of conduct. Airlines can define behaviors that are sufficient for denying a customer service. But control rights are not absolute. A property owner cannot allow white place users to engage in one form of behavior but ban Asians and Blacks from doing the same.

Exclusion: The right to keep people out *Exclusion*, the term used by both Kenton (2020) and Schlaeger and Ostrom (1992), is the right to ban entry onto the property. Johnson (2015) incorporates this right in his "right to possess." This right allows an owner to ban trespassing and helps keep homes private. Businesses could not set opening and closing hours without this right. This right undergirds the place management function, control of access.

But it is not an unrestricted right. In the 1960s, civil rights activists convinced the courts and society that owners of public businesses could not restrict access based on race. The Americans with Disabilities Act limits how property owners can exclude individuals with mobility and other limitations (Burgdorf, 1991; Johnson, 2015).

Entry: The right to allow others onto the property Entry is another right that gives place managers the ability to control access. It gives owners the right to allow people to come onto the property. Honore' (1961) and Johnson (2015) include this right within the right they call *manage*, along with several other rights. This right becomes obvious when it is restricted. Public housing officials have often restricted which tenants can enter their units. In our rented units, neither Shannon nor John can have guests for more than a few days unless they receive permission from their landlord.

Withdrawal: The right to income from rents, profits, and other sources We are using the term used by Schlaeger and Ostrom (1992) although Honore' (1961) and Johnson (2015) call this the right to income. Leases and rental agreements usually involve one party giving the owner money in exchange for conferring some rights to that property. This right also allows an owner to sell timber from her property and enjoy income from other extraction. The owner has the rights to that money. This right is one of several that make meaningful the place management function acquisition of resources.

But owners do not have the right to income to any activity. If an owner operates an illicit drug dealing operation on the property, the state can seize the property and the income from the illicit activity.

Security: The right to retain ownership and be free of expropriation Security (Honore', 1961; Johnson, 2015) also supports acquisition of resources. This right prohibits seizing the property against the will of the owner. However, this very basic right has limits. If a homebuyer purchases a place with a bank loan, the bank can seize the property if the buyer fails to pay back the loan with interest on the schedule the buyer and bank agreed to. Failure to pay taxes is another way this right evaporates.

Alienation: The right to sell, consume, waste, or destroy An owner usually has the right to sell the property, use it up, waste, or destroy it. Legal theorists give it several names—*capital* (Honore', 1961; Johnson, 2015) or *disposition* (Kenton, 2020)—but we use the name favored by Schlaeger and Ostrom (1992). In addition to profiting from using a property for a business, owners may profit from the rise in value of the property. This right protects the owner's access to the increase in value. But owners do not have to seek to increase the property's value. They could allow the property to deteriorate, unless doing so violates health and safety regulations.

Not all sticks in the bundles described in papers on property rights have direct connections to the ORCA functions, so we will not describe them here. One of these sticks, however, is important for understanding place management in general.

Contract: The right to contract for the use of property We have defined place managers as people (or institutions) who own and operate property or those to whom owners have delegated authority. One way to delegate property rights is to contract with another person or institution to act on behalf of the property owner. So an owner of an apartment complex may contract with a management firm to operate the complex. Or an owner can lease property for uses the lessee would like to undertake. A building's owner might lease the ground floor of his building to a bar, for example, and rent the floors above to a start-up tech firm. Honore' (1961) incorporates this right in his more general right to manage. But it deserves separate mention because the right to delegate authority can be separated from the other rights within management.

Delegation may take other forms. An owner may employ people to carry out her rights to control, alter, exclude, or entry. An owner can accept the services of volunteers to do the same. Absent a conveyance of property rights—direct or delegated—a person cannot carry out the full range of place management functions. However, in circumstances where property rights are ambiguous, unenforced, or highly contested, it is possible for nonowners to act as place managers. Shantytowns and areas inhabited by squatters are such circumstances (Neuwirth, 2006).

Fig. 4.1 Property rights, place management, and explanations

Figure 4.1 shows links between property rights and place management. Each of the place management functions is connected to one or more rights. The rights give place managers the authority to undertake actions within each of the ORCA functions.

Authority, Power, and Social Control

What gives the owners of these rights authority and power? There is a long debate over this matter, but for practical purposes it is the fact that the person who possesses these rights can have them enforced by a court of law. A right without recourse to law has no teeth, as the US Supreme Court understood when it ruled on the invalidity of racial covenants.

A racial covenant is a restriction in the right of an owner to sell or rent property to people classified as being of a particular race, religion, or ethnic group. These covenants were common throughout the United States, as well as Canada and Great Britain, in the first half of the twentieth century (Gotham, 2000). Real estate developers included them in the deeds of new homes on the theory that white buyers would pay a premium to know that Black, Jewish, or other people of other excluded groups would not live in the neighborhood (Glotzer, 2020). If the neighborhood was already established, homeowners had to organize. If a substantial proportion of homeowners agreed (thus restricting their rights to alienation), then all properties in an area would contain these restrictions (Rose & Brooks, 2016). If a Black or Jewish family purchased a house with such a restriction, then neighbors could sue to evict them, and ownership would revert to the previous owner.

The US Supreme Court, in *Shelley v. Kraemer* (334 U.S. 11948), ruled that if a court ruled in favor of neighbors contesting a sale based on a racial covenant, the court would be facilitating racial discrimination. Consequently, the Supreme Court declared that lower courts could not enforce these covenants. In the absence of state powers, the use of racial covenants declined, until outlawed by the US Congress in 1968 (Rose & Brooks, 2016).

Shelley v. Kraemer illustrates that place management powers depend on the courts. They are not informal. This is why a landlord can evict a tenant, why a business owner can create and enforce rules of behavior, and why the police cannot enter people's property without a warrant. Finally, property rights explains why almost all crime prevention at places are place management interventions. Even if it is the police who promote these measures, without place managers carrying them out, they cannot be applied.

We can now complete formula (4.2), giving us a complete definition of place management.

$$(X) \text{Property owners, and their delegates,} (A) \text{apply ORCA functions on their property to guide} (T) \text{place users} (G) \text{ to achieve place} - \text{specific goals,} (P) \text{using one or more of their rights to property.} \qquad (4.4)$$

Table 4.1 compares informal social control and place management for each of the variables necessary to define a control mechanism. In each case, place management is substantially different from informal social control. (X) Place managers are owners of property or people to whom owners have delegated rights. They may or may not be local residents, the basic requirement of informal social control actors. (A) Place management actions are extremely broad, as defined by the ORCA functions. In contrast, informal social control actions are best summarized as guardianship, something place managers can apply but do not have to. (T) The targets of place management are people who use a place, regardless of age or place or residence. The targets of informal social control are usually young people living in the neighborhood. (G) The goals of place managers are the smooth functioning of the place, sometimes for profit but often for other purposes. Control of crime and disorder is seldom a goal. Informal social control is largely about preventing crime or disorder. (P) Finally, place management derives its powers from the law of property rights. If

Table 4.1 Differences between informal social control and place management

	X: actors	A: actions	T: targets	G: goals	P: powers
ISC	Community residents	apply guardianship	over community youth	to prevent crime	using (vague)
PM	Property owners and their delegates	apply ORCA functions on their property to guide	place users	to achieve place specific goals	using property rights

Generic formula: X does A to T to achieve G, using P

a dispute about these powers arises, the disputants can ask a court to resolve it. The powers residents can use to create informal social control are unclear.

We made three points in this chapter. First, informal social control is a fuzzy concept. Even if it is made less fuzzy, it does not seem to have the power required to make much impact on serious crime. Second, place management is not informal social control. It differs from informal social control at least five ways (Table 4.1). Third, place management authority to exercise control is strong, tangible, and recognized in law. Its roots are in the willingness of the state to define and enforce property rights.

If place managers have these powers to control behaviors on their properties, why do some places have so much crime? In the next chapter, we try to answer that question.

References

Alchian, A. A., & Demsetz, H. (1973). The property right paradigm. *The Journal of Economic History, 33*(1), 16–27.

Burchfield, K. B. (2009). Attachment as a source of informal social control in urban neighborhoods. *Journal of Criminal Justice, 37*(1), 45–54.

Burgdorf, R. L., Jr. (1991). The Americans with Disabilities Act: Analysis and implications of a second-generation civil rights statute. *Harvard Civil Rights-Civil Liberties Law Review, 26*(2), 413–522.

Carr, P. J. (2003). The new parochialism: The implications of the beltway case for arguments concerning informal social control. *American Journal of Sociology, 108*(6), 1249–1291.

Glotzer, P. (2020). *How the suburbs were segregated: Developers and the business of exclusionary housing, 1890–1960*. Columbia University Press.

Gotham, K. F. (2000). Urban space, restrictive covenants and the origins of racial residential segregation in a US city, 1900–50. *International Journal of Urban and Regional Research, 24*(3), 616–633.

Greenberg, S. W., & Rohe, W. M. (1984). Perspectives neighborhood design and crime: A test of two perspectives. *Journal of the American Planning Association, 50*(1), 48–61.

Groff, E. R. (2015). Informal social control and crime events. *Journal of Contemporary Criminal Justice, 31*(1), 90–106.

Honore', A. M. (1961). Ownership. In A. G. Guest (Ed.), *Oxford essays in Jurisprudence* (pp. 370–375). Oxford University Press.

Johnson, D. R. (2015). Reflections on the bundle of rights. *Vermont Law Review, 32*(2), 247–272.

Kenton, W. (2020). Bundle of rights. *Investopedia*. October 30. https://www.investopedia.com/terms/b/bundle-of-rights.asp. Accessed 9 July 2021.

Kubrin, C. E., & Weitzer, R. (2003). New directions in social disorganization theory. *Journal of Research in Crime and Delinquency, 40*(4), 374–402.

Linning, S. J., Olaghere, A., Eck, J. E., & Steinman, H. (2022). What is informal social control? A review of the criminology literature, 2010-2020. Presentation at the Conference of the American Society of Criminology, Atlanta, GA, November 16.

Merrill, T. W., & Smith, H. E. (2010). *Property*. Oxford University Press.

Nash, J. K., & Bowen, G. L. (1999). Perceived crime and informal social control in the neighborhood as a context for adolescent behavior: A risk and resilience perspective. *Social Work Research, 23*(3), 171–186.

Neuwirth, R. (2006). *Shadow cities: A billion squatters, a new urban world*. Routledge.

Reynald, D. M. (2009). Guardianship in action: Developing a new tool for measurement. *Crime Prevention and Community Safety: An International Journal, 11*(1), 1–20.

Rose, C. M., & Brooks, R. R. W. (2016). Racial covenants and housing segregation, yesterday and today. In A. Brown & V. Smith (Eds.), *Race and real estate* (pp. 161–176). Oxford University Press.

Sampson, R. J., Raudenbush, S. W., & Earls, F. (1997). Neighborhoods and violent crime: A multilevel study of collective efficacy. *Science, 277*(5328), 918–924.

Sargeant, E., Murphy, K., McCarthy, M., & Williamson, H. (2021). The formal-informal control nexus during covid-19: What drives informal social control of social distancing restrictions during lockdown? *Crime & Delinquency.* https://doi.org/10.1177/0011128721991824

Schlager, E., & Ostrom, E. (1992). Property-rights regimes and natural resources: A conceptual analysis. *Land Economics, 68*(3), 249–262.

Schulenberg, J. L. (2016). Police decision-making in the gray zone: The dynamics of police–citizen encounters with mentally ill persons. *Criminal Justice and Behavior, 43*(4), 459–482.

Silver, E., & Miller, L. L. (2004). Sources of informal social control in Chicago neighborhoods. *Criminology, 42*(3), 551–584.

Warner, B. D. (2014). Neighborhood factors related to the likelihood of successful informal social control efforts. *Journal of Criminal Justice, 42*(5), 421–430.

Wickes, R., & Hipp, J. R. (2018). The spatial and temporal dynamics of neighborhood informal social control and crime. *Social Forces, 97*(1), 277–308.

Wickes, R., Hipp, J. R., Sargeant, E., & Mazerolle, L. (2017). Neighborhood social ties and shared expectations for informal social control: Do they influence informal social control actions? *Journal of Quantitative Criminology, 33*(1), 101–129.

Chapter 5
Place Manager Failures and Successes

Why Some Fail But Most Do Not

That crime gets in the way of place managers achieving their desires suggests all place managers would suppress crime. Given their considerable powers, why do some place managers allow a great deal of crime on their properties? In this chapter, we address this question by using a typology of place managers and by describing the role of super controllers. Then we discuss the costs of crime and who bears these costs. In most circumstances, crime is sufficiently costly that there are strong incentives to fight crime. For a relatively few place managers, particularly if they do not bear crime costs, it is easier or more useful to tolerate crime.

Controls on Place Managers

The first priority of all place managers is the functioning of their place. Whether it is a family home, an apartment building, a store, bar, or bowling alley, crime is usually a headache rather than the central concern. How much of a headache depends on the type of crime, the chance of crime occurring, the costs crime imposes on place managers, and the costs of doing something about it (relative to alternative ways of spending money, time, and effort).

Notice the difference between place managers' incentives and those of guardians and handlers (Chap. 2). Guardians and handlers are defined by their crime control functions. The former protect targets from theft or damage. The latter protect nascent and experienced offenders from themselves. Place managers' primary role is to attend to place functioning. If crime does not get in the way of place functioning, is a relatively minor impediment, or enhances it, place managers will ignore it. If crime does get in the way, they will attempt to do something to prevent it, if the prevention costs are not too high. In addition, place managers can fail due to incompetence, misinformation, inexperience, corruption, and other reasons.

But much place management failure to address crime may be intentional: it's not worth the effort. If a place manager can achieve his goals without attending to crime, he may ignore crime. Perrow (1984) makes a similar case about industrial accidents. Zero tolerance for crime is rare.

How a place manager responds to crime is a choice. Tamara created a typology of place managers based on whether they are active or passive managers and whether they attempt to reduce crime or allow it. *Suppressors* are active managers who suppress crime. They take steps in anticipation of a crime threat. They do not tolerate crime. *Reactors* are more passive in their management style. If a crime occurs, they will act to prevent future occurrences, but they will not incur prevention costs without strong evidence it is necessary. *Enablers* also adopt a passive management style, but do little to prevent future crime on their properties, even following a crime event. They are crime tolerant. Finally, *promoters* actively manage their places in ways that encourage crime. They gain from criminal activity (Eck & Madensen, 2018, p. 278). These differences, we suspect, are due to incentives rather than personalities. So let's look at where incentives to attend to crime might come from.

Two types of incentives influence place managers' choices. The first is self-interest. For the control of crime, in many circumstances, this is enough for a place manager to be a suppressor or reactor. But there are incentives imposed from the outside by what Rana Sampson and colleagues (2010) call super controllers. Super controllers are people, organizations, and institutions who control the behavior of guardians, handlers, and place managers. They provide incentives to address crime and disincentives for ignoring or facilitating crime.

Rana Sampson and her colleagues (2010) examined a wide variety of circumstances where police addressed crime-prone circumstances and had to induce place managers, guardians, or handlers to improve their crime prevention activities. They discovered the police sometimes enlisted the support of fourth parties (generally, parties one and two are the victim and offender; a third party is the place manager, guardian, or handler). They organized these fourth parties into three categories, each with two or more subcategories. And they called these fourth parties *super controllers* because they exercise control over primary controllers (guardians, handlers, and managers). We show this relationship in Fig. 5.1.

Formal super controllers have some legal connection to controllers. Financial institutions include banks, insurance companies, and other organizations to which a place manager has a financial agreement. Regulatory agencies have powers to compel or prohibit place management activities. The sales of alcohol, for example, are tightly regulated. Zoning regulation controls the types of activities a place manager can undertake at his place. Some place managers are employees of organizations, and so their employer has some formal control over their activities. Other place managers are contractors to an owner. A company owning apartment buildings may contract with another company to operate one or more of their buildings, for example. A national restaurant chain may not own any of its restaurants, but works with franchisees to own and operate the places in the name of the chain. Finally, courts may intervene and direct place managers on how to behave. The top panel in Table 5.1 illustrates how these formal super controllers vary over three different types of places.

Diffuse super controllers are usually not specific organizations. They are institutions made up of multiple organizations and individuals. Formal super controllers

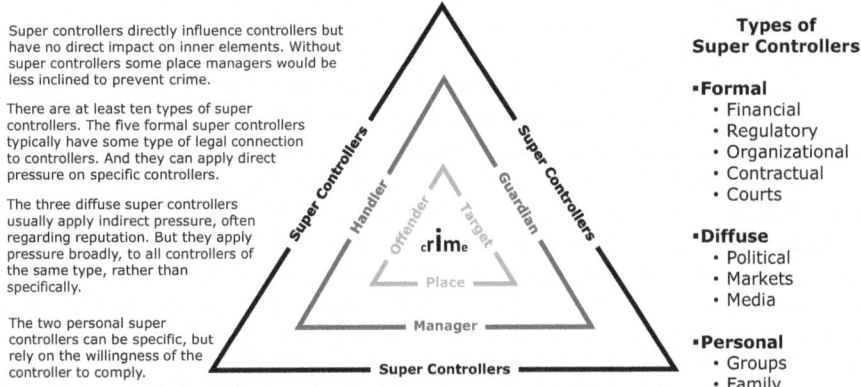

Fig. 5.1 Routine activity theory's triangles with super controllers. (See Sampson et al. (2010))

Table 5.1 Examples of super controllers for three types of places

	Single-family home	Apartment building	Bar or pub
Formal			
Financial	Mortgage holder, insurance company	Lenders, insurance companies	Lenders, insurance companies
Regulatory	Local zoning	Health and safety, housing authority	Alcohol Beverage Control Authority
Organizational		Owner and superintendent	Owner and manager
Contractual	Owner and landscaper	Owner and management company	Franchiser
Courts		Premises liability suits	Premises liability suits
Diffuse			
Political		Pressure on regulators	Pressure on regulators
Markets	Real estate market	Rental market	Reputation among customers
Media		Press attention	Reputation among customers
Personal			
Groups	Neighbors	Landlord associations	Associations of bar owners Area merchants associations
Family	Relatives		

focus on specific place managers with whom they have a legal connection. Diffuse super controllers paint with a wide brush. They can affect the reputation of places, their market values, or their vulnerability to formal super controllers. Political super controllers may threaten to hold hearings. Political inquiries may draw the attention of formal regulators or result in laws creating regulations. Hearings might draw in media super controllers who publicize repugnant activities at a place. Markets for the goods or services provided by some places may be affected, thus impinging on the acquisition of resources (see middle panel in Table 5.1).

The third large category of super controllers are personal. For some place managers, peer businesses or neighbors might be salient. For others, family members might be important. Personal super controllers do not have the authority of formal super controllers, but they can be more focused than diffuse super controllers. Another distinguishing feature is that personal super controller actions are often hidden from view. Industry groups often publish, for their members, voluntary standards of best practice. Peer place managers can be sources of advice. But the public seldom hears about a place manager admonishing her deviant peer for ignoring best practices. This is because they have their conversation behind closed doors.

Failures

With all these controls and the fact that crime is harmful, why would any proprietary place have repeated incidents of crime? Singular events can be explained easily by peculiar circumstances or momentary lapses. But after such events, we would expect place managers to take steps to prevent the recurrence of crime. Why do a few place managers appear to be crime tolerant?

Let us start by looking at the types of losses crime can create. To keep this simple, we will consider three broad categories of loss:

1. *Direct losses* due to crime: theft of goods, damage to the place, injuries to place users, attacks on place managers, or psychological losses from trauma.
2. *Reputational losses*: potential place users avoid coming to the place due to fear or repugnance.
3. *Prevention costs*: expenditures of time and effort to prevent additional crimes.

After a crime occurs, only the third is under the control of place managers. However, some mitigation of reputational losses is possible (e.g., paying off place-user victims and requiring nondisclosure agreements). The costs vary by crime type—a theft of a small item has little direct cost and no reputational cost, but an injury to a customer imposes large direct and reputational costs, for example.

Direct losses are not all born by the place manager. In his study of catastrophic accidents, Charles Perrow (1984, p. 67) provides a useful four-level typology of those who bear the costs. We will adapt it to the study of crime places. Level 1 includes place managers—including owners, employees, volunteers, and other operators. We will divide this first level into (1a) owners and (1b) employees and

Table 5.2 Who bears the costs of crime at places?

Cost type	Level 1		Level 2	Level 3	Level 4
	Owners	Employees, etc.	Place users	Others nearby	Taxpayers
Direct	X	X	X	X	X
Reputation	X				
Prevention	X	X	?		X

contract workers. At level 2 we have place users such as customers, clients, delivery people, and others who voluntarily entered the place to take advantage of a place's functions. Level 3 bearers of crime costs include people passing by the place, neighbors, and others who are not using the place but who share the same environment with the place (in Chap. 6 we look at this in detail). Perrow (1984) has a fourth level, future generations, because he is dealing with accidents that can harm fetuses and alter the genetic makeup of future generations. Extremely few crimes create these effects, so we will redefine level 4. For us, level 4 contains people who bear the monetary costs of coping with crimes that directly affect others, namely, taxpayers.

The three types of costs are not distributed equally (Table 5.2). Although direct costs impact any level, reputational costs are born by the owner, mostly. Prevention costs are centered on level 1. If the proprietary place sells goods or services to place users, the place manager may be able to pass some of the prevention costs to them, through increased prices. But this only works if place users are relatively insensitive to price. For this reason, we have a question mark regarding place users bearing prevention costs. However, taxpayers (level 4) often bear increased policing and other government costs. Importantly, the types of costs are not independent. If the owner bears a high direct cost and a high reputational cost, she is probably more likely to spend time, effort, and money to avoid the first two costs. On the other hand, an owner who does not feel the direct costs and perceives no reputational cost is unlikely to spend much on prevention. In some circumstances, an owner can shift prevention costs to taxpayers, thus gaining a hidden subsidy (a topic we discuss in Chap. 9).

Consider the following hypothetical examples, each based on real cases observed by the authors:

1. A very large retailer develops a business plan based on low personnel costs and volume sales. Theft prevention reduces volume sales and increases personnel costs. Most shoppers are unaware of shoplifting and are not directly affected by it. So theft can be tolerated as long as it is within normal bounds. The retailer focuses on deterrence as a prevention strategy to arrest many shoplifters, turning them over to the local police.
2. An owner of an apartment building tolerates drug dealing in its premises because the dealer reliably pays his rent in cash. Other renters have few choices for alternative living places. The regional public housing authority continues to refer subsidized renters to the building. So the owner does not suffer from reputational loss. Police handle some, though not all, of the crimes associated with the drug dealing.

3. A nightclub gains a reputational advantage among people who enjoy its music and the easy access to recreational drugs. The costs of breaking up fights are born by bouncers and give the place an attractive edgy reputation. The occasional shooting creates temporary drops in business. Police investigate the serious incidents they hear about and sometimes make arrests.
4. Thieves routinely break into vehicles parked in a pay lot. The owner and employees are unaffected. As parkers do not communicate among each other, the reputation of the lot does not suffer. Parking is scarce, so there are always customers. Police take reports from vehicle owner victims, but make few arrests due to the lack of clues.
5. An elderly owner of a single-family home allows her nephew to live in her house. The nephew engages in drug dealing from the house, with the consequence that thefts increase in the surrounding area. Disputes between the dealer-nephew and users sometimes result in fights or shootings. The owner values her duty to her kin above her reputation in the neighborhood and suffers no direct costs. Police respond to some of the incidents stemming from these activities, although the owner never calls the police.
6. Fights in a local park give the park a reputation for being unsafe, so few people use it. The city parks department is unaware of its reputation and indifferent to the residents of the neighborhood. Residents of the neighborhood do not know how to register their unhappiness with the parks department, but they do call the police. In response, police step up patrols in the park. These result in some negative police-citizens encounters, some arrests, and some allegations of police discriminatory enforcement.
7. A used-car dealership suffers repeated vehicle thefts. The thefts are due to poor control over vehicle keys and to insurance fraud. Customers are unaware of this, so the dealer suffers no loss to his reputation. The dealer's insurance company pays off his claims, if it receives a police report. So the dealer demands his employees to call the police, thus causing detectives to spend time investigating the reported thefts.
8. A shelter for homeless men has frequent fights due to cramped conditions and inadequate staffing. The nonprofit running the shelter does not want to improve the physical setting or hire more staff. Charitable donors are unaware of the fights and injuries to shelter users because the shelter's managers do not inform donors. Police frequently come to handle the fights.
9. The owner of a convenience store makes most of his money through laundering money for local drug sellers. He recruits some drug users to steal from nearby merchants and trades drugs for the stolen merchandise, which he sells to others. Shoplifting and street robberies in the surrounding blocks increased when he started operations. The dealers and users who hang out nearby occasionally get into disputes resulting in shootings. Police intensively patrol the area surrounding the store and make some arrests. The police drug unit occasionally launches undercover operations. But these are expensive and fail to stop the criminal activity for very long.

10. A man routinely beats his wife in the shared apartment they lease. A property management company owns the building but the company's representative does not have an office there. Other tenants are unaware of the assaults. The landlord is unaware of damage to walls and flooring in the apartment. The building's reputation as a safe, convenient, and comfortable location is unsullied. These assaults are never reported to the police.

Place management failures

A boarded two-family house. The graffiti was old when this picture was taken in spring, 2021. The boards suggest that someone had some interest in managing it. But the graffiti, untrimmed grass, and upper floor broken window suggests the management is weak. By the fall of 2022, the owner had renovated the place.

An abandoned building on a former military base. When the U.S. Navy left this base, they deeded part of their land to the town. The town could not find a way to develop the place, or protect it. With no active place management, people removed all the metal wiring and many pipes. Teens use some of the structures to hang out.

11. A motel chain focuses on the low-income segment of its market. As a result, compared to other motel chains, it has a larger proportion of its clientele who get into trouble—trash rooms, fight with other guests, and engage in illicit behaviors. The chain's parking areas are unprotected, resulting in vehicle break-ins. The chain employs fewer staff at each motel, pays them less, and trains them less than other chains. Consequently, the staff are likely to overlook misbehavior, take bribes, or engage in misbehavior. The chain has a poor reputation, but those who use their motels cannot afford other motels. The owners are sheltered from the misbehavior, though their employees are sometimes threatened or injured. Police routinely take reports from employees and motel guests and make some arrests.

In each case, crime repeatedly occurs but the owners are sheltered from some crime costs. Sometimes the costs are relatively minor relative to other gains (the large retailer, nightclub, and motel chain). Sometimes the place manager is also an offender (used-car dealership, convenience store, and shared apartment), but mostly the place manager is not. Sometimes the costs are serious, but are born by employees, place users, others in the area, or taxpayers (single-family home and park). Sometimes the reputation of the place suffers, but the owner is indifferent or even benefits (the apartment building, nightclub, and motel chain). In other cases, potential place users and others are unaware of the crimes, so the place's reputation is unaffected (the used-car dealership, parking lot, and homeless shelter). In almost all cases, police have to respond to the place's crimes. This means that taxpayers bear part of the costs of the place's operation.

In each case, the place manager is free of relevant super controllers. The donors to the homeless shelter, for example, could pressure the nonprofit to protect its clients better, but are ignorant. If regulators attentive to crime existed—analogous to health regulators who monitor restaurants or inspectors who monitor workplace safety—then the place managers for the motel, very large retailer, apartment building, convenience store, and parking lot would have greater incentives to curb crime (see Chap. 9).

In short, it is difficult for place managers to make crime pay for them, but when they can, their place operations create high-crime locations. Sometimes they can make crime pay because it impacts others far more than owners and the costs to owners are trivial relative to cost savings from giving crime prevention a low priority. Like the landlord who ignores plumbing leaks, holes in the roof, and electrical malfunctions because she has difficulty making a profit, a place manager may ignore crime too. Sometimes place managers can profit directly from crime. Sometimes place managers are incapable of dealing with crime or are unaware of it, even though they bear much of the costs. Though uncommon, place managers in any area may operate this way. However, low-income areas inhabited by people who are cut off from the mainstream economy and political process will have more such place managers than high-income areas well connected to politicians and government officials (Eck, 2019).

Conclusions

In our hockey stick graph (Fig. 1.2 in Chap. 1), we sorted places into three categories according to where they fell along a continuum of crime involvement. We can now give explanations for why some places are at one part of the continuum and others are in another part.

Places without crime for long periods are alike in that they do not permit the routine convergence of offenders and targets, either because offenders do not go there, targets are not present, or targets are too well protected.

There are several explanations of places with very few crimes: those in the middle of the hockey stick handle. First, offenders occasionally make mistakes. They try to commit a crime at a place that is largely immune to crime (e.g., does not have the relevant targets) and they do not come back. Second, a place that is usually not vulnerable to crime has a temporary lapse in normal precautions. After the crime, place managers restore normal precautions. Third, a vulnerable place is discovered by offenders, but before they can commit many crimes, place managers adjust the physical and social environment to prevent repeats.

This leaves us with the relatively few high-crime places on the blade of the hockey stick. These places routinely facilitate crime, and super controllers are insufficiently powerful to change them. There are probably many ways a place can be vulnerable to crime, just as production systems can break down in many ways. Importantly, after one or two crimes signal to the place manager the vulnerability, the place manager does not act effectively to prevent future crimes.

To paraphrase Leo Tolstoy's first line in *Anna Karenina*, crime-free places are all alike; every crime-prone place is crime prone in its own way. But crime-prone places do have one thing in common: their place managers are not doing much about the crime because they have weak incentives to do much. In Chap. 9, we examine ways to create stronger incentives. But before we do so, we examine ways crime places can radiate crime beyond their boundaries (Chaps. 6 and 7) and ways safe places can spread safety into their surrounding environments (Chap. 8).

References

Eck, J. E. (2019). Race, place management, and crime. In J. D. Unnever, S. L. Gabbidon, & C. Chouhy (Eds.), *Building a black criminology: Race, theory, and crime* (pp.171–206). Routledge.

Eck, J. E., & Madensen, T. D. (2018). Place management, guardianship, and the establishment of order. In D. S. Nagin, F. T. Cullen, & C. L. Jonson (Eds.), *Deterrence, choice, and crime: Contemporary perspectives* (pp. 269–296). Routledge.

Perrow, C. (1984). *Normal accidents: Living with high-risk technologies*. Basic Books.

Sampson, R., Eck, J. E., & Dunham, J. (2010). Super controllers and crime prevention: A routine activity explanation of crime prevention success and failure. *Security Journal, 23*(1), 37–51.

Chapter 6
The Extended Place Manager I: Crime Radiation

Introduction

Until now, we have treated crime at places as if they were like Las Vegas; the misbehavior at a place stays at the place. But is this true? Features of a place that promote crime within it may also radiate crime in its surroundings. This chapter challenges the Las Vegas assumption.

We call the area into which a place radiates crime its *purlieu* (two of us pronounce it pearl-loo, but our Canadian coauthor suggests pearl-lee-ou). Why a new name for an area when we already have neighborhood, community, and environment? First, we wanted a term that does not imply residents, social connections, or other criminological concepts. Second, a purlieu is a characteristic of a proprietary place but these older terms suggest something else. An analyst establishes the place first and then marks out its purlieu (left panel in Fig. 6.1). In contrast, with the terms neighborhood, community, environment, and area, an analyst first establishes the region and then locates the places within its boundaries (right panel in Fig. 6.1).

Finally, a purlieu is similar to a buffer (Ratcliffe, 2012) but a buffer is an analytical tool used to estimate a purlieu. A purlieu is a theoretical idea. If an analyst suspects a place has a purlieu, she may use a series of buffers to determine if it does. Although it is handy to think of a purlieu as circular or rectangular with the place at its center, purlieus come in all sorts of shapes, depending on street patterns and other area feature. Crime could radiate along a street in one direction from a high-crime place, for example. It need not radiate along all streets in all directions. Therefore, we will use *purlieu* to describe the region into which a place might create crime. When our subject is a region, we use the word *area*.

This equation summarizes this chapter's topic: $C = P + U$. The number of crimes within the borders of a proprietary place is P. The total crime produced by the place is C. Until this chapter, we have assumed that $C=P$. In this chapter, we consider the possibility that the place creates crimes outside of its boundaries. The number of

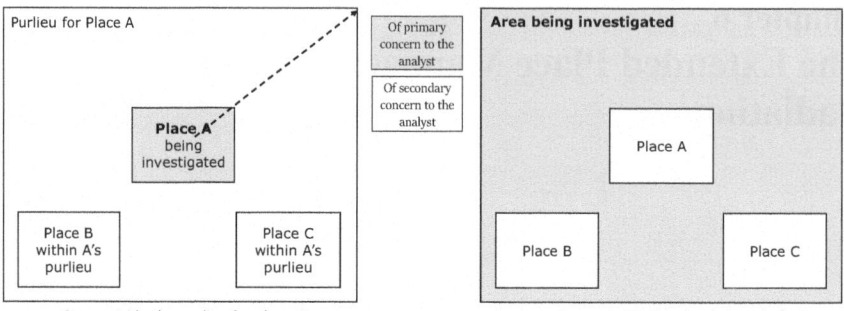

Fig. 6.1 Place, purlieu, and area

crimes radiated into its purlieu is U. We try to answer the most basic question, is U greater than zero? Do high-crime places radiate crime into their surroundings?

In the next section, we will examine the large body of research that suggests that some facilities radiate crime. There is considerable research on this topic. Still, there are good reasons for treating these studies with skepticism.

The third section examines the diffusion of crime control benefits—the opposite of crime displacement. Diffusion implies radiation. We argue that the evidence for diffusion give us better reason for taking radiation seriously.

Then we turn to a study that directly tackles our topic. Here we find clear evidence of crime radiation. If studies were singers, this study would be the lead singer, and the studies we examine in the two earlier sections would be backup vocalists. Because the lead singer and backup vocalists are in harmony, we have reason to believe that crime places may radiate crime. Nevertheless, there are many unanswered questions.

Do Some Facilities Radiate Crime to Their Purlieus?

Wanting to answer the question, why do some areas have more crime than other areas, researchers have asked if the types of facilities within areas are an answer. The first researchers designed their studies like the right panel in Fig. 6.1. Recently, researchers have used buffers to estimate purlieus for these facilities, like the left panel in Fig. 6.1.

Drinking places have an unsavory reputation. They can bring into neighborhoods customers who, once drunk, are either convenient victims or belligerent offenders. They may trigger either mechanism. It is no wonder that social scientists have asked whether bars, taverns, pubs, and other alcohol outlets increase crime within their areas.

The first study, in the Canadian city of Edmonton, found that areas containing or near drinking places had more crime than similar areas without drinking places (Engstad, 1975). Other studies in other cities—Minneapolis, USA (Frisbie et al., 1977); Cleveland, USA (Roncek & Bell, 1981; Roncek & Maier 1991); Newcastle upon Tyne, UK (Hope, 1985); San Diego, USA (Roncek & Pravatiner 1989); and Philadelphia, USA (Groff 2014; Groff & Lockwood 2014)—confirmed the first impression.

Crime researchers branched out to other facilities. Table 6.1 lists 13 facilities that research has associated with crime in their surroundings. You should exercise caution in reading this table. We did not conduct a systematic review: there are studies we did not include that show similar results. More important, we only included studies showing positive effects on crime—to demonstrate crime radiation is a possibility. We did not enumerate every crime radiating facility; nail and hair salons and churches, for example, are sometimes found to be associated with crime nearby (Irvin-Erickson, 2015) as are tobacco shops (Subica et al., 2018). And we do not show findings for broad categories of facilities—businesses, industrial plants, and so forth (Boessen & Hipp, 2015).

Even with these cautions, the variety of facilities that seem to radiate crime is impressive. Researchers measured the crime areas around a facility in a number of ways: counties, census tracks and blocks, street segments, and others. Some of the more recent research applies variable buffers to estimate purlieus. They defined boundaries at increasing distances from the facility so they can count crimes within 500 meters, 1000 meters, or 1500 meters (or whatever distances they choose). Often, the radiating effect declines from inner to outer buffers. Jerry Ratcliffe (2012), for example, estimates that the average violent crime purlieu for Philadelphia's 1282 bars is about 85 feet (almost 26 meters). Beyond this, bars have little impact on violence. This decline in crime as the distance from the facility grows points to the facility as the source of the trouble.

Although crime may radiate from these facilities, how much crime they radiate depends on the type of facility, time of day, distance from facility, social economic characteristics, age of business (Kim et al., 2022), and a host of other conditions (Blair et al., 2017; Block & Block, 1995; Haberman et al., 2011; Haberman & Ratcliffe, 2015; Stucky & Smith, 2017; Taniguchi & Salvatore, 2012).

Many of the studies compare the crime in areas with a facility to other areas without the facility. If the area with the facility has more crime than the areas without it, then researchers assume it's the facility causing the difference. Even when researchers control for other characteristics of the neighborhood, we are looking at an association not an explicit causal connection. There are at least five reasons we need to be cautious in how we interpret these findings.

First, the increase in area crime may be due to the crime within the facility rather than crime radiated into the area. A bar with many fights inside, but none outside,

Table 6.1 Facilities increasing crimes in their areas

Facility	Study	Increases crime in its ...
Abandoned buildings, vacant properties, foreclosed buildings	Oliphant (2021) Porter et al. (2019)* Raleigh and Galster (2015)	Variable buffers Street segments Census blocks
Alcohol outlets—bars, taverns, pubs, and licensed establishments	Bernasco and Block (2011) Groff (2014) Haberman et al. (2011) Oliphant (2021)	Census blocks Street segments Variable buffers Variable buffers
Bus stops	Liu et al. (2020)* Oliphant (2021)	Buffers up to 200 meters Variable buffers
Casinos	Grinols and Mustard (2006)* Lan et al. (2021)*	County 400-meter buffer
Convenience stores	Bernasco and Block (2011) Haberman and Ratcliffe (2015) Oliphant (2021)	Census blocks Census blocks Varied distances
Fast-food restaurants	Askey et al. (2018) Bernasco and Block (2011) Haberman and Ratcliffe (2015)	Street blocks Census blocks Census blocks
Fringe financial shops—payday loan, pawn, check cashing	Bernasco and Block (2011) Haberman et al. (2011) Haberman and Ratcliffe (2015) Kubrin and Hipp (2016)	Census blocks Variable buffers Census tracts Census blocks
Schools	Haberman et al. (2011) LaGrange (1999)	Variable buffers Census enumeration areas
Illegal markets—drug, prostitution, gambling	Haberman and Ratcliffe (2015) Rengert et al. (2005)	Census blocks Census block groups
Parks	Groff and McCord (2011) Haberman and Ratcliffe (2015)	Variable buffers Census blocks
Public housing (USA)	Aliprantis and Hartley (2015)* Haberman et al. (2011) Holloway and McNulty (2003)	Census block groups Variable buffers Census block groups
Social assistance—homeless shelters, drug treatment	Haberman et al. (2011) Haberman and Ratcliffe (2015) Moyer and Ridgeway (2020)*	Variable buffers Census blocks Variable buffers
Subway stops	Bernasco and Block (2011) Haberman et al. (2011) Haberman and Ratcliffe (2015)	Census blocks Variable buffers Census block

*Examined crime before and after opening of facility

will increase area crime, even though it does not radiate fights. Studies that use census or city blocks, street segments, or other areas are particularly difficult to interpret. The studies using variable buffers centered on facilities can give stronger evidence of crime radiation.

Second, these findings seem to be too much of a bad thing (Wilcox & Eck, 2011). It is difficult to find a type of facility that does not create trouble for its area. With so many troublesome facilities, maybe we should look for something common to all of the facilities rather than assume there is something criminogenic about each specific facility.

Third, a prime candidate for a common feature may be that all these facilities are on busy streets. Facilities locate on busy streets because it enhances their business (Brantingham & Brantingham, 1995; Wilcox & Eck, 2011). Crime follows the traffic. In short, busy street segments generate crime, not the specific facilities on the street. Research shows that the busyness of streets is a large predictor of crime in an area (Bernasco & Block, 2011; Block & Block, 1995; Deryol et al., 2016; Tillyer & Walter, 2019). And other research demonstrates that street patterns influence area crime levels (Greenberg & Rohe, 1984; Summers & Johnson, 2017; Tarkhanyan, 2014). A few of the facilities studies do control for traffic volume or street size (Stucky & Ottensmann, 2009), but most do not.

Fourth, most of the studies cannot show which came first, the crime or the facility. Would their conclusions be different if the studies looked at changes in crime from before to after the facility opened? When John MacDonald et al. (2018) looked at schools, before and after opening, they found no evidence that schools increase crime in their vicinity, in contrast to the school studies reported in Table 6.1. Examining openings does not always change our conclusions, however. Ruth Moyer and Greg Ridgeway (2020) examined the impact of the opening and closing of drug treatment centers on crime in the centers' purlieus. Their findings were consistent with the findings of other less rigorous studies. In Table 6.1, we mark with asterisks (*) the few studies that looked at opening and closing.

The final problem with these studies is that they appear to contradict the hockey stick distribution of crime. It is hard to imagine a world where crime is distributed across sites like a hockey stick, but where all facilities radiate an equal amount of crime into their environment. It is more likely that facilities with many crimes inside would radiate more crime to their purlieus than facilities with little or no inside crime. Despite findings that parks are crime prone, for example, Cory Eybergen and Martin Andresen (2022) find that only a few parks have crime problems, and most parks have little crime. The findings of many of the studies listed in Table 6.1 may be the result of a few extremely high-crime places rather than typical places.

To reconcile the findings from studies in Table 6.1 with the hockey stick findings, YongJei Lee et al. (2021) considered how place management might influence findings. They examined 18 different types of facilities (column 1 in Table 6.2) in Cincinnati over several years. With multiple years of data, they could account for openings and closings of facilities. They first replicated earlier research, such as Stucky and Ottensmann (2009). Of the 18 facilities, 13 were associated with inflated crime levels (Table 6.2, second column). Since some property owners owned two or

Table 6.2 Management of facilities matters

Facility (in decreasing order of association with crime, before removing management effects)	Association with crime	After ownership Effects removed	
		Change	Association
Fast food	+	▼	+ ?
Retail shops	+	▼	+
Restaurants	+	▼	+ ?
Apartments	+	▼	+
Hotels	+	▼	+ ?
Bars	+	▼	+ ?
Car service centers	+	▼	+ ?
Schools	+	▼	+ ?
Offices	+	▼	+ ?
Hospitals	+	▼	+ ?
3 + family homes	+	▼	+
Warehouses	+	▼	+ ?
Two family homes	+	▼	+
Worship places	−	▲	+ ?
Garages	−	▼	−
Universities	+ ?	▲	− ?
Vacant lands	−	▼	−
Single-family homes	−	▲	−
Total positive and significant	13 of 18		4 of 18

Based on Lee et al. (2021)
Key
+ positive association with crime
− negative association with crime
? nonsignificant association with crime
▲ association increased after removing ownership effects
▼ association decreased after removing ownership effects

more of the facilities in the dataset, Lee and his team adjusted the analysis to account for common ownership. Their new results showed declines in the association between crime and facilities for the 15 facilities previously shown to be associated with crime (column 3). Now only 4 of original 13 facilities demonstrated significant crime (column 4).

These findings suggest that much of the crime associated with facility types is due to the way owners manage their facilities. Fast-food places may cause crime in their areas, for example, not because there is something crime-causing about fast-food sales, but because a few fast-food restaurants are managed in ways that foster crime.

It is possible that poorly managed places that produce crime create harm within their purlieus. The evidence cannot rule out this possibility. But the flaws in the evidence leave considerable uncertainty.

The Diffusion of Crime Control Benefits and Its Implications

People unfamiliar with crime-place research often ask, if you prevent crime at a place, won't the crime just move to other places nearby? The people asking this question assume that crime will *displace*—shift its location—and the displaced crime is equal to the crime prevented, so there is no net gain from place-based prevention. This is like assuming offenders are similar to bugs or rats: criminal activity is so much a part of them that they cannot stop offending, so they go elsewhere. Is displacement inevitable?

No, it is not. From the 1980s through the early 2000s, researchers have examined the evidence for displacement (Bar & Pease, 1990; Bowers et al., 2011; Cornish & Clarke, 1987; Eck, 1993; Guerette & Bowers, 2009; Hesseling, 1994; Telep et al., 2014). All these reviews of the scientific research on displacement came to the same conclusions. First, often displacement did not occur; it is not inevitable. Second, displacement is not typical; most studies show no detectable displacement. Third, the volume of displaced crime is almost always less than the volume of crime prevented. In one study, researchers and police tried to create displacement. Despite considerable effort and the use of multiple displacement measurement tools, they found little displacement (Weisburd et al., 2006).

So, displacement can occur, but it is not inevitable or even highly likely. High-crime places, therefore, do not protect nearby places by sucking in the crime. And nearby places are not under an inevitable threat from preventing crime at hot places. This does not mean high-crime places radiate crime into their surroundings, although this research leaves open the door to crime radiation.

A body of research related to displacement studies does imply crime radiates from high-crime locations into their purlieus. In the mid-1990s, Ronald Clarke and David Weisburd (1994) pointed out that crime prevention efforts sometimes make their target location safer and reduce crime in the areas surrounding the place. This is the opposite of displacement. Clarke and Weisburd called this phenomenon the diffusion of crime control benefits, or *diffusion* for short.

One reason for diffusion may be that high-crime places attract offenders; they are destinations. On the way to or from their destinations, offenders notice crime opportunities in the surrounding areas. If the high-crime place did not attract offenders, offenders would not travel through the purlieu, would not notice the crime opportunities, and would not commit crimes in the purlieu.

In short, high-crime places are analogous to large anchor stores in shopping districts. An anchor store attracts large numbers of customers, some of whom then shop at smaller retailers nearby. When an anchor store closes, its customers no longer go to the smaller nearby stores. Perhaps, high-crime places are *crime anchor points*. When crime preventers drive down crime at a crime anchor point, fewer offenders go to it. So, like shoppers, they no longer visit nearby locations. They miss the crime opportunities in the purlieu they would have seen, and so crime goes down in the purlieu. Perhaps this is what produces the diffusion of benefits.

Places influence their surroundings

Stadia are large proprietary places but are seldom in use. They can have a large influence on activities within their purlieus. On a rare game day, the area around this football stadium is extremely active.

Over a decade after Clarke and Weisburd's (1994) insight, sufficient evaluations had accumulated that researchers could undertake a systematic review of diffusion to determine if it was rare or common. They found that diffusion, much like displacement, is not inevitable, but it is slightly more likely than displacement (Bowers et al., 2011; Guerette & Bowers, 2009).

From the diffusion research, we can be confident that troublesome places may be crime anchor points that radiate crime into their purlieus. Because diffusion is variable, crime radiation may be variable—some high-crime places will radiate a great deal of crime, others will radiate no crime, and other crime places will radiate modest amounts of crime.

Direct Evidence for Radiation

The diffusion research provides evidence that high-crime places may radiate crime to nearby locations. It is indirect because radiation is an implication that logically follows from the diffusion research, but radiation is not a specific finding of any diffusion study.

Kate Bowers (2014) provides direct evidence. She set out to determine if hot places became hot because they were in high-crime areas or if hot places increased the crime in their purlieus. The difficulty she faced was that it is relatively simple to demonstrate that crime at a place is correlated with crime in its surroundings, but it is far more difficult to determine which direction crime flows: from outside the place to inside or from inside to outside.

Bowers examined 4 years of reports to police of theft-from-persons reports—over 30,000 cases—in the center of a large British city. These include snatches (3%

of the thefts)—the offender grabs an item and dashes off; pickpocketing (24%); and stealing of unattended property in workplaces, drinking places, cafés, or open spaces (73%).

She determined if the theft occurred inside a property (72% of thefts) or outside. After she divided the city center into squares, 50 meters on a side, she assigned each theft to its square based on location data. She also assigned inside thefts to their address. So for each square, she had a count of thefts inside businesses and outside businesses.

Bowers found that the more high-inside-crime places in a square, the more outside crime occurred in the square. Although the volume of inside crime seemed to influence the volume of outside crime, it was the number of high-inside-crime places that mattered most. Because Bowers was able to document which came first, the high-crime places or the outside crimes, she could eliminate the possibility that crime flowed from the outside into places.

This result is consistent with the results from the diffusion research. Bowers' research implies that if place managers were able to reduce the number of high-crime places, the thefts in the areas outside the businesses would go down.

Conclusions

Are places like Las Vegas? Do crimes stay within the places that create them? We have reviewed three collections of studies that imply the answer is no. The first set of studies shows that some types of facilities appear to increase crime nearby. For reasons we discussed, this is probably the weakest body of evidence for crime radiation. The second body of research—diffusion of crime control benefits—is stronger. We can be more confident that changes in the crime site had an impact on crime in the site's surrounding environment. Further, because sites for crime prevention tend to be sites with high-crime levels, we have indirect evidence that high-crime places radiate crime into their purlieus. Finally, we have a single study that directly investigates crime radiation. This study finds that the more high-crime places in an area, the greater the crime outside these places.

Although we would like to have more studies that directly investigate crime radiation, with the evidence we have, we can be reasonably confident that crime radiation occurs. Exactly how common, exactly how much radiation of what types of crime, and exactly how far the radiation extends, we do not know.

The evidence is insufficient for academic researchers to draw strong conclusions. But academic researchers can wait for future evidence because they do not have to act now. Those who fight crime—as government agents, as business owners, or as community activists—have to create plans now, based on the evidence we have now. Our advice is they should act as if the high-crime places with which they are grappling are radiating some crime: assume that crime places are not like Las Vegas, crime happening inside may not stay inside.

In the next two chapters, we examine two other ways places influence crime in their surroundings. Chapter 7 looks at networks among crime-involved places and how these may create violent crime hot spots. Chapter 8 looks at networks of safety. That chapter shows how real estate investors and developers can spread safety throughout an area.

References

Aliprantis, D., & Hartley, D. (2015). Blowing it up and knocking it down: The local and city-wide effects of demolishing high concentration public housing on crime. *Journal of Urban Economics, 88*(July), 67–81.

Askey, A. P., Taylor, R., Groff, E., & Fingerhut, A. (2018). Fast food restaurants and convenience stores: Using sales volume to explain crime patterns in Seattle. *Crime & Delinquency, 64*(14), 1836–1857.

Barr, R., & Pease, K. (1990). Crime placement, displacement and deflection. In M. Tonry & N. Morris (Eds.), *Crime and justice: A review of research* (Vol. 12, pp. 277–318). University of Chicago Press.

Bernasco, W., & Block, R. (2011). Robberies in Chicago: A block-level analysis of the influence of crime generators, crime attractors, and offender anchor points. *Journal of Research in Crime & Delinquency, 48*, 33–57.

Blair, L., Wilcox, P., & Eck, J. E. (2017). Facilities, opportunity, and crime: An exploratory analysis of places in two urban neighborhoods. *Crime Prevention & Community Safety, 19*(1), 61–81.

Block, R. L., & Block, C. R. (1995). Space, place and crime: Hot spot areas and hot places of liquor-related crime. In J. E. Eck & D. Weisburd (Eds.), *Crime and place* (pp. 145–183). Criminal Justice Press.

Boessen, A., & Hipp, J. R. (2015). Close-ups and the scale of ecology: Land uses and the geography of social context and crime. *Criminology, 53*(3), 399–426.

Bowers, K. J. (2014). Risky facilities: Crime radiators or crime absorbers? A comparison of internal and external levels of theft. *Journal of Quantitative Criminology, 30*(3), 389–414.

Bowers, K. J., Johnson, S. D., Guerette, R. T., Summers, L., & Poynton, S. (2011). Spatial displacement and diffusion of benefits among geographically focused policing initiatives: A meta-analytical review. *Journal of Experimental Criminology, 7*(4), 347–374.

Brantingham, P. J., & Brantingham, P. L. (1995). Criminality of place: Crime generators and crime attractors. *European Journal of Criminal Policy & Research, 3*(1), 5–26.

Clarke, R. V. G., & Weisburd, D. (1994). Diffusion of crime control benefits: Observations on the reverse of displacement. In R. V. G. Clarke (Ed.), *Crime prevention studies* (pp. 165–183). Criminal Justice Press.

Cornish, D. B., & Clarke, R. V. G. (1987). Understanding crime displacement: An application of rational choice theory. *Criminology, 25*(4), 933–947.

Deryol, R., Wilcox, P., Logan, M., & Wooldridge, J. (2016). Crime places in context: An illustration of the multilevel nature of hot spot development. *Journal of Quantitative Criminology, 32*(2), 305–325.

Eck, J. E. (1993). The threat of crime displacement. *Criminal Justice Abstracts, 25*(3), 527–546.

Engstad, P. A. (1975). Environmental opportunities & the ecology of crime. In R. A. Silverman & J. J. Teevan (Eds.), *Crime in Canadian society* (pp. 193–211). Butterworth.

Eybergen, C., & Andresen, M. A. (2022). Public parks and crimes of property: Get out there and enjoy the sunshine, lock your cars, and hide your bike. *Security Journal, 35*(3), 777–800.

Frisbie, D., Fishbine, G., Hintz, R., Joelsons, M., & Nutter, J. B. (1977). *Crime in Minneapolis: Proposals for prevention*. Minnesota Governor's Commission on Crime Prevention and Control.

Greenberg, S. W., & Rohe, W. M. (1984). Neighborhood design and crime: A test of two perspectives. *Journal of the American Planning Association, 50*(1), 48–61.

References

Grinols, E. L., & Mustard, D. B. (2006). Casinos, crime, and community costs. *The Review of Economics & Statistics, 88*(1), 28–45.

Groff, E. R. (2014). Quantifying the exposure of street segments to drinking places nearby. *Journal of Quantitative Criminology, 30*(3), 527–548.

Groff, E. R., & Lockwood, B. (2014). Criminogenic facilities and crime across street segments in Philadelphia: Uncovering evidence about the spatial extent of facility influence. *Journal of Research in Crime & Delinquency, 51*(3), 277–314.

Groff, E. R., & McCord, E. S. (2011). The role of neighborhood parks as crime generators. *Security Journal, 25*(1), 1–24.

Guerette, R. T., & Bowers, K. J. (2009). Assessing the extent of crime displacement and diffusion of benefits: A review of situational crime prevention evaluations. *Criminology, 47*(4), 1331–1368.

Haberman, C. P., Groff, E. R., & Taylor, R. B. (2011). The variable impacts of public housing community proximity on nearby street robberies. *Journal of Research in Crime & Delinquency, 50*(2), 163–188.

Haberman, C. P., & Ratcliffe, J. H. (2015). Testing for temporally differentiated relationships among potentially criminogenic places and census block street robbery counts. *Criminology, 53*(3), 457–483.

Hesseling, R. B. P. (1994). Displacement: A review of the empirical literature. In R. V. G. Clarke (Ed.), *Crime prevention studies* (pp. 197–230). Criminal Justice Press.

Holloway, S. R., & McNulty, T. L. (2003). Contingent urban geographies of violent crime: Racial segregation and the impact of public housing in Atlanta. *Urban Geography, 24*(3), 187–211.

Hope, T. (1985). *Implementing crime prevention measures*. Her Majesty's Stationery Office.

Irvin-Erickson, Y. (2015). *Identifying risky places for crime: An analysis of the criminogenic spatiotemporal influences of landscape features on street robberies*. Unpublished dissertation, Rutgers, The State University of New Jersey, New Brunswick.

Kim, Y.-A., Wo, J. C., & Hipp, J. R. (2022). Estimating age-graded effects of businesses on crime in place. *Justice Quarterly*. https://doi.org/10.1080/07418825.2022.2107943

Kubrin, C. E., & Hipp, J. R. (2016). Do fringe banks create fringe neighborhoods? Examining the spatial relationship between fringe banking and neighborhood crime rates. *Justice Quarterly, 33*(5), 755–784.

Lan, M., Liu, L., & Eck, J. E. (2021). A spatial analytical approach to assess the impact of a casino on crime: An example of Jack Casino in downtown Cincinnati. *Cities, 111*(February), 103003. https://doi.org/10.1016/j.cities.2020.103003

LaGrange, T. C. (1999). The impact of neighborhoods, schools, and malls on the spatial distribution of property damage. *Journal of Research in Crime & Delinquency, 36*(4), 393–422.

Lee, Y., O, S.-H., & Eck, J. E. (2021). Why your bar has crime but not mine: Resolving the land use and crime – Risky facility conflict. *Justice Quarterly, 39*(5), 1009–1035.

Liu, L., Lan, M., Eck, J. E., & Kang, E. L. (2020). Assessing the effects of bus stop relocation on street robbery. *Computers, Environment & Urban Systems, 80*(March). https://doi.org/10.1016/j.compenvurbsys.2019.101455

MacDonald, J., Nicosia, N., & Ukert, B. (2018). Do schools cause crime in neighborhoods? Evidence from the opening of schools in Philadelphia. *Journal of Quantitative Criminology, 34*(3), 717–740.

Moyer, R. A., & Ridgeway, G. (2020). The effect of outpatient methadone maintenance treatment facilities on place-based crime. *Journal of Experimental Criminology, 16*(2), 227–245.

Oliphant, S. N. (2021). Examining time-variant spatial dependence of urban places and shootings. *Journal of Urban Health, 98*(6), 777–790.

Porter, L. C., De Biasi, A., Mitchell, S., Curtis, A., & Jefferis, E. (2019). Understanding the criminogenic properties of vacant housing: A mixed methods approach. *Journal of Research in Crime & Delinquency, 56*(3), 378–411.

Raleigh, E., & Galster, G. (2015). Neighborhood disinvestment, abandonment, and crime dynamics. *Journal of Urban Affairs, 37*(4), 367–396.

Ratcliffe, J. H. (2012). The spatial extent of criminogenic places: A changepoint regression of violence around bars. *Geographical Analysis, 4*(4), 302–320.

Rengert, G. F., Ratcliffe, J. H., & Chakravorty, S. (2005). *Policing illegal drug markets: Geographic approaches to crime reduction*. Criminal Justice Press.

Roncek, D. W., & Bell, R. (1981). Bars, blocks, and crimes. *Journal of Environmental Systems, 11*(1), 35–47.

Roncek, D. W., & Maier, P. A. (1991). Bars, blocks, and crimes revisited: Linking the theory of routine activities to the empiricism of "hot spots". *Criminology, 29*(4), 725–753.

Roncek, D. W., & Pravatiner, M. A. (1989). Additional evidence that taverns enhance nearby crime. *Sociology & Social Research, 73*(4), 185–188.

Stucky, T. D., & Ottensmann, J. R. (2009). Land use and violent crime. *Criminology, 47*(4), 1223–1264.

Stucky, T. D., & Smith, S. L. (2017). Exploring the conditional effects of bus stops on crime. *Security Journal, 30*(1), 290–309.

Subica, A. M., Douglas, J. A., Kepple, N. J., Villanueva, S., & Grills, C. T. (2018). The geography of crime and violence surrounding tobacco shops, medical marijuana dispensaries, and off-sale alcohol outlets in a large, urban low-income community of color. *Preventive Medicine, 108*(April), 8–16.

Summers, L., & Johnson, S. D. (2017). Does the configuration of the street network influence where outdoor serious violence takes place? Using space syntax to test crime pattern theory. *Journal of Quantitative Criminology, 33*(2), 397–420.

Taniguchi, T. A., & Salvator, C. (2012). Exploring the relationship between drug and alcohol treatment facilities and violent and property crime: A socioeconomic contingent relationship. *Security Journal, 25*(2), 95–115.

Tarkhanyan, L. (2014). *Urban design and drug crime: Uncovering the spatial logic of drug crime in relation to the urban street network and land use mosaic in London*. Unpublished dissertation, University College London, London.

Telep, C. W., Weisburd, D., Gill, C. E., Vitter, Z., & Teichman, D. (2014). Displacement of crime and diffusion of crime control benefits in large-scale geographic areas: A systematic review. *Journal of Experimental Criminology, 10*(4), 515–548.

Tillyer, M. S., & Walter, R. J. (2019). Busy businesses and busy contexts: The distribution and sources of crime at commercial properties. *Journal of Research in Crime & Delinquency, 56*(6), 816–850.

Weisburd, D., Wyckoff, L. A., Ready, J., Eck, J. E., Hinkle, J. C., & Gajewsk, F. (2006). Does crime just move around the corner? A controlled study of spatial displacement and diffusion of crime control benefits. *Criminology, 44*(3), 549–592.

Wilcox, P., & Eck, J. E. (2011). Criminology of the unpopular. *Criminology & Public Policy, 10*(2), 473–482.

Chapter 7
The Extended Place Manager II: Hidden Crime-Involved Places and Place Networks

You can't hit what you can't see.
– Walter Johnson, baseball pitcher

Captain Maris Herold was in trouble. The mayor and chief of police had asked her to create a violence reduction strategy for Cincinnati. They tossed the responsibility in her lap because she led a successful violence reduction strategy at one of the city's worst violence hot spots. Captain Herold was a big advocate for place-based interventions and had used them repeatedly. She knew that the violence reduction tactics she tried on a particularly violent hot spot had worked well. They worked well for 90 days, but violence returned. She was out of ideas.

Captain Herold poured out her concerns to Tamara. Tamara had pioneered research into places that facilitate crime elsewhere. Some places did not experience crime themselves so they would not always show up in crime data. She wondered if identifying such places could help the captain. She asked Captain Herold about three types of hidden places within the violent hot spot. The captain grabbed a napkin and Tamara's pen. She drew a map of the visible and invisible places connected to the violence. Looking at Captain Herold's sketch, Tamara asked, "Did failing to address those invisible places allow violence to return? If we created a city-wide strategy that addresses hidden places, could we reduce violence for longer?"

Introduction

In this chapter we describe the research that led to Tamara's questions and the new violence reduction strategy that followed. The ideas discussed here are on the leading edge of crime place research and practice. Like our discussion of crime radiation (Chap. 6) and discussions in the following chapters, we have sufficient evidence to be encouraged, but insufficient evidence to claim we have nailed down the truth.

We have been discussing proprietary places with a great many crime events connected to the property. These are the crime places we find in police databases, the places crime analysts show on maps, and the places researchers study. We can talk about them with great confidence because data reveals them. But there are crime-involved places data does not reveal. Hidden crime places are one subject of this chapter.

We have been discussing high-crime places as separate parcels. In this and the next chapter, we will discuss how places connect to one another. Good place networks we leave until Chap. 8. In this chapter, our other subject is bad networks.

We have not emphasized methods for reducing crime at high-crime places. When we have mentioned practical ways to fight place-based crime, we have done so in passing. Starting in this chapter, we put more emphasis on policy and practice, culminating with Chap. 9.

We start by introducing three types of hidden crime-involved places. These are the kinds of places Tamara asked Captain Herold about. Hidden crime-involved places may help explain why violent crime hot spots are hard to suppress. Visible and hidden crime places form networks that support violent hot spots. This is the topic of our second section. The failure to address the network of crime-involved places allows violence to return. If this is true, then what should we do? The answer to this question is the subject of the third section. Here we describe place network investigations (PNI) and explain how this strategy reduces violence by applying networked place theory principles. The last section is our conclusion to this chapter.

Place Types and Crime Functions

Cincinnati Police Sergeant Matt Hammer investigated drug trafficking and specialized in intelligence gathering to identify people moving drugs to street corners. He was also a master's student taking John's graduate course in crime prevention. The course troubled Sergeant Hammer. In none of John's lectures, in none of the class discussions, and in none of the readings had Matt found a mention of places drug traffickers use to stash their drugs, weapons, or money. There was no discussion of the places traffickers used to relax, drink, and have a good time. And there was no discussion of places offenders used to surveil their neighborhood, identify threats, and spot targets. Yet Hammer had investigated such places.

In class, Sergeant Hammer asked a question; "What do we know about the hidden places offenders use to facilitate their criminal activities? These places will not show up in researchers' crime data, but they are important." John had never thought of such places, so he did what all professors do. He asked Hammer to write his class paper on the topic. Hammer's (2011) paper, on what he called *comfort spaces*, would lead to insights into crime places and to a violence reduction strategy.

Shortly after Hammer submitted his paper, Tamara and John began writing a book chapter summarizing the work on crime places. They decided to create a typology of places. We have mentioned their distinction between proprietary, proximal, and pooled places. Here we discuss their distinctions among four types of proprietary places (Madensen & Eck, 2013).

Crime Sites

Crime sites are places where crimes occur. These are the types of proprietary places we have discussed in Chaps. 1, 2, 3, 4, 5, and 6. Crimes occur at these sites, and some of these crimes are reported to police, who record these events in their databases. Reporting and recording make them visible. Because they are visible, analysts can show them on crime maps and can depict crime hot spots, as small as a proprietary place and as large as several city blocks. Visibility allows us to draw the hockey stick crime curve we showed in Fig. 1.2.

Convergence Settings

Convergence settings are public places where potential offenders meet. Marcus Felson (2003) coined this term. Offenders use convergence settings in a variety of ways: including recreating with friends, meeting new people, recruiting accomplices, exchanging information, planning future offenses, and selling stolen goods. While some of these activities are criminal (e.g., selling stolen goods), other activities are not. All activities are consensual, so few of them attract police attention.

Hidden crime involved places

These two pictures are of buildings on opposite sides of a street segment.

This recently renovated apartment building is not involved in crime.

Unrenovated and boarded apartment buildings. One of these places contains a comfort space, according to police investigators.

Convergence settings are open to the public. Any proprietary place where people gather can serve as a convergence setting: a transit hub, nightclub, a shopping center, or park, for example. By design they bring all manner of people together. Most convergences in these settings are legitimate and socially useful. We suspect that most convergence settings are not crime involved, but a few are highly crime involved. For example, Gisela Bichler, Aili Malm, and Janet Enriquez (2014) call places that facilitate the congregation and frequent interaction of delinquent youth *magnetic locations*.

Convergence settings are less likely than crime sites to appear in police data. Meetings among offenders are seldom crimes and no one reports them. Police seldom hear about consensual exchanges of stolen goods, drugs, guns, and money. The offenders have good reasons to avoid serious criminal behavior because that would draw police attention. Other place users are either unaware of the presence of offenders or do not care. Although convergence settings have lower profiles than crime sites, they do occasionally come to police attention. This may occur when the people who converge get into violent disputes.

Comfort Spaces

In contrast to convergence settings, Hammer's *comfort spaces* are private. Comfort spaces are offender-controlled, nonpublic places. Offenders, their relatives, friends, or other associates own them. Comfort spaces can be houses or apartments. Some are inside of businesses: the backroom of a convenience store, for example.

Hammer (2011) suggested that comfort spaces serve three functions. Some are hideouts where offenders can chill with their friends. They are rest and relaxation places. Second, offenders sometimes use comfort spaces to hide goods, drugs, money, and other things from other offenders and from the police. Human traffickers use them to hide people. Third, offenders use some comfort spaces as staging locations to prepare for their next crime. Offenders may choose them because they have sight lines useful for spotting likely targets or police.

To protect comfort spaces from police scrutiny, offenders avoid committing observable crimes at these sites. Thus, comfort spaces seldom appear in police crime data. However, like convergence settings, police and community members are often aware of comfort spaces.

Police discover comfort spaces through the course of investigations aimed at disrupting illicit markets and violent group activity. Specialized units, like Hammer's violent crime squad, focus on uncovering these locations by covertly monitoring offenders' movements. Informants may mention them. Undercover police may follow known offenders to these places. Watchful community members are also aware of comfort spaces, particularly when such places attract unusual foot traffic at odd hours.

Corrupting Spots

The fourth type of place used by offenders is the *corrupting spot* (Madensen and Eck, 2013). Corrupting spots are proprietary places that stimulate crime at other locations. They usually operate as legitimate businesses. Metal recycling yards buying stolen copper pipe, antique shops buying and reselling stolen merchandise, pharmacies illegally dispensing controlled substances, convenience stores engaging in money laundering, and automobile repair shops buying and installing stolen catalytic converters are examples of corrupting spots that increase crime in their purlieus.

Table 7.1 Hidden crime-involved places

Facility type	Involvement in offender activities	Crime place type
Community park	Provides surveillance opportunities to oversee nearby weapon exchanges	Convergence settings
Parking lot	Permits gatherings for dice games behind an unsecured dumpster	
Neighborhood bar	Encourages recreational interactions between local offenders	
Vacant property	Offers refuge for offenders and associates	Comfort spaces
Apartment unit	Facilitates nearby illegal interactions by allowing space to store illicit goods	
Grocery store stockroom	Allows offenders to hang out and offers an escape route if detected by police	
Tire shop	Enables dumping of hazardous materials and buys/sells stolen vehicle parts	Corrupting spots
Convenience store	Sells keys to nonresidents to access a pool in a gated apartment complex	
Cell phone repair shop	Launders money associated with a local open-air drug market	

Before the rise of the Internet, we would end our description with the physical places. Today, however, many corrupting spots are *virtual* places. Social media sites that fail to screen posts and advertisements act as virtual corrupting spots, promoting criminal activity across the Internet.

As the crimes at corrupting spots are largely consensual, these criminal acts are rarely reported to police. Investigators sometimes hear of corrupting spots but have insufficient evidence to close them. Property crime investigators may find that many investigations end at a metal recycler. Investigators of organized crime may identify money-laundering fronts. In a neighborhood Shannon studied, a convenience store served as a corrupting spot by laundering money and by tasking drug addicts to steal goods from local stores. Police knew this spot and spent years trying to close it, before they were successful (Linning & Eck, 2021).

We call the four types of crime places CS^4. As part of her research, Tamara asked police officers to describe their encounters with hidden CS^4 places. Their answers, summarized in Table 7.1, show the variety of the three hidden crime places.

Networked Places and Violent Crime Hot Spots

Captain Herold was able to sketch a map of the CS^4 connected to her violent crime hot spot because police were aware of these locations. But until her discussion with Tamara, the significance of this place knowledge was unappreciated. By naming and describing them, Tamara had prompted Captain Herold to diagram the crime place infrastructure of a violent hot spot.

We have avoided using the term *hot spot* until this chapter because it is ambiguous. Researchers put the label hot spot on any geographic concentration of crime:

address, street segment, a few streets, neighborhoods, and larger areas. We use the term to label a cluster of crime larger than a proprietary place but not larger than a few square blocks. Captain Herold's hot spot was smaller than a square block.

The durability, or persistence, of violent hot spots is a major problem for violence reduction strategies. This is why Thomas Abt (2019) calls violence *sticky*. To illustrate stickiness, Tamara likes to ask officers two questions when she rides with them. First, "Where should I hangout if I want to get mugged tonight." Officers typically respond by speeding to a violent location. Second, "How long has this location been this way?" Regardless of time in service—1 year or 30—officers respond by saying, "For my entire career." Some crime hot spots are chronic, persistent generators of crime. Why?

The answer may have to do with how offenders act before, during, and after their crimes. We tend to think of crime as an event, occurring at a crime site. But crime is a process that started before the event and continues after. Because it's a process, offenders need multiple places, and the CS^4 places describe their basic needs. Consider the hypothetical offender moving from place to place in Fig 7.1. Almost all of his activities involve hidden crime places.

It occurred to Tamara and Captain Herold that when a crime place's infrastructure remains intact, it is easy for a crime hot spot to bounce back from an effective prevention effort. Offenders do not displace and build a new crime infrastructure elsewhere; that requires too much effort and takes too much time. Instead, they wait. When police shift their attention to other problem locations, offenders return and make use of the intact infrastructure. A crime place network makes violence sticky at hot spots.

The left diagram in Fig. 7.2 shows a cleaner version of the network Captain Herold drew on a napkin (we deal with the right diagram later). When Captain Herold identified it in 2016, the hot spot created by the network was the city's most

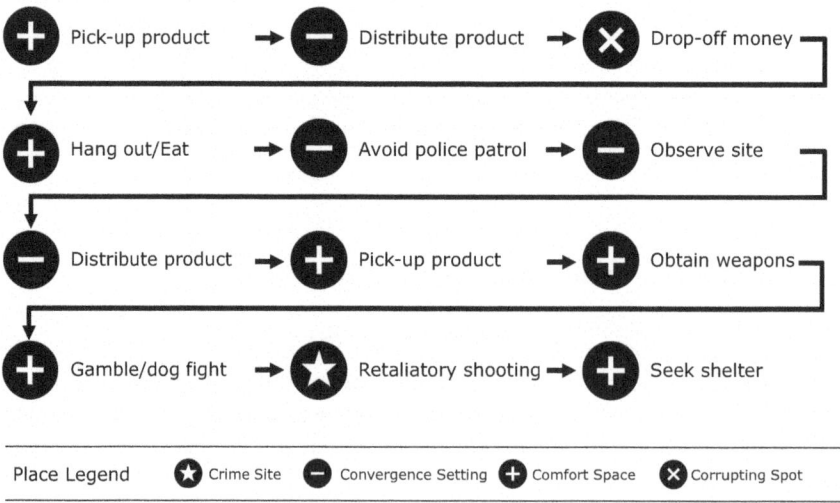

Fig. 7.1 Movement within an offender place network

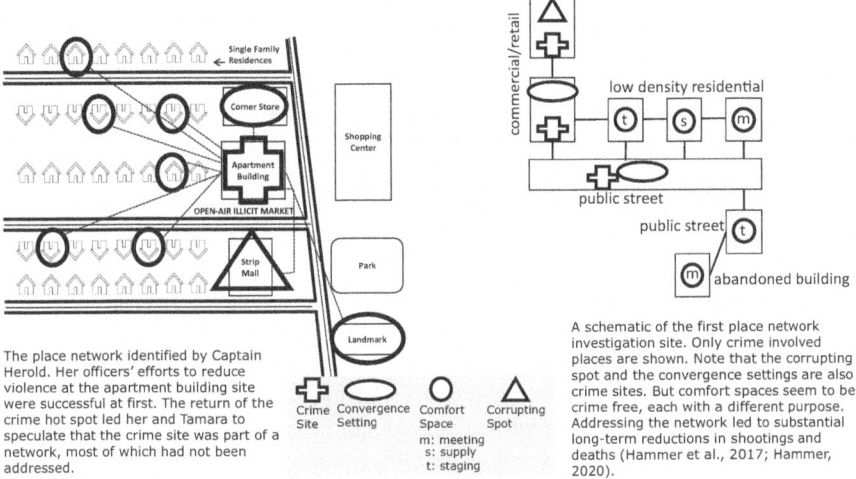

Fig. 7.2 Crime place networks

violent. At its center was an aging apartment building. A young street gang ran an open-air drug and weapon sales just south of the apartment building. Gang members used two convergence settings: a corner market that provided cover and shelter and a community landmark that allowed higher-ranking members to monitor market activities without being present during illicit exchanges. A single landlord rented several houses to gang members. The gang members used these comfort spaces to stage their crimes and store their supplies. A few nearby businesses served as corrupting spots. Two businesses in a nearby strip mall purchased stolen goods from people who wished to buy drugs or weapons. These businesses also laundered money for the gang members. Although considered one of the most crime-ridden locations in Cincinnati, most other nearby places experienced little to no crime and were not involved in the place network. Even within the strip mall, only two of the stores were part of the network.

Tackling Crime-Involved Place Networks

Tamara assisted Captain Herold to develop a place network violence reduction strategy. Although Captain Herold left the Cincinnati Police to become chief of the University of Cincinnati Police, the Cincinnati Police Department adopted her strategy.

Place Network Investigations (PNI)

The strategy began with a careful study of violence locations. Rather than spread resources over neighborhoods, police identified 23 tiny areas, each spanning approximately two square blocks. These hot spots made up only 1.4 percent of the city's land mass, but accounted for more than 14 percent of all serious crime, 26 percent of violent crime, and 43 percent of all shooting victims (Madensen et al., 2017). These tiny areas also accounted for disproportionally large numbers of police officer injuries.

Next, police selected two areas for pilot test of the strategy. The police department assigned skilled investigators to uncover place networks. Investigators interviewed patrol officers, specialized units, city and social service personnel, and community members. Officers worked with crime analysts to understand crime and victimization patterns. They identified people and place connections through surveillance activities, both covert and overt. Officers used these techniques to reveal place functions—whether specific places served as crime sites, convergence settings, comfort spaces, corrupting spots, or some combination (e.g., a business that served as a corrupting spot, but also generated large numbers of calls-for-service). Encounters with noncooperative place managers sometimes required talking to business employees, security officers, and confidential informants to build civil and criminal cases against place owners. The right diagram of Fig. 7.2 depicts the place network behind the violence at the first pilot place network investigation site.

Although police spearheaded the investigations, a board determined which actions were used to dismantle the network. On the board were community leaders and representatives of city agencies. This assured that a range of options were considered, that local residents' and business' interests were not overlooked, and that the people who could take action were part of the planning. The board reviewed the investigative findings, observed the crime hot spot, and used data from their agencies to identify other possible hidden crime places. The board offered recommendations and allocated resources to dismantle the network.

The actions made by the board went beyond traditional police crime suppression tactics. The board chose a variety of crime blocking tactics depending on the place under scrutiny. These tactics included revoking business licenses through civil remedies, legislating new management practices, mandating employee training, requiring structural building changes, or complete property abatement. The board had the city demolish vacant buildings, alter traffic patterns, move public transit locations, repair blighted property, increase lighting, and initiate community development projects. If possible, the board tried to switch the use of places in positive ways: turning an empty field into a community center or converting a corrupt convenience store into an inexpensive used clothing store, for example (see Herold and Eck, 2020).

Table 7.2 illustrates the range of organizations, departments, and community participants who assisted in altering the violence infrastructure of the first place-based investigation site. The network contained nine places (A through I) but each needed its own solution. This is why, with the exception of the police, no organization worked on all places and why each place has a distinct array of organizations. Some organizations provided overall guidance for the entire network, while most provided place-specific assistance. Three of the 14 partners—building inspection, law department, and health department—have regulatory powers over places and are place manager super controllers.

Place network investigations contain a strong analytical component. One reason is that analysts need to bring together investigators' information to create network diagrams and monitor the size and shape of the violence hot spot. Another is that the board needs to scrutinize crime trends to track progress. Analysts looked at the numbers of shootings and other violent acts each week, and they looked at the days between shootings. The more days between shootings, the more effective the effort (Hammer et al., 2017).

Based on innovation, evidence of effectiveness, and community collaboration, the Center for Problem-Oriented Policing awarded the Cincinnati Police Department's place network approach the 2017 Herman Goldstein Award for Excellence in Problem-Oriented Policing (Hammer et al., 2017).

Place Network Investigations Evidence

In 2020, Matt Hammer, by then a lieutenant, evaluated the impacts of Cincinnati's first five place-based inventions. All sites showed declines in shooting, averaging 50%, but varying across the sites (from 12 to 90 percent). Displacement was limited

Table 7.2 Organizations involved in reducing violence at the first PNI site

Partners	Site-wide	Place within place network								
		A	B	C	D	E	F	G	H	I
Police	X	X	X	X	X	X	X	X	X	X
Community leaders	X	X			X	X	X	X		X
Building inspections		X	X	X		X	X		X	
Economic development	X					X	X			X
Traffic engineering										
Public works department	X									
Law department			X			X		X		
Partnering center	X									
Keep Cincinnati Beautiful	X									
Violence reduction leaders	X					X	X			
Health department						X				
Recreation Commission										X
County probation	X									
Private partners	X									X

Adapted from Hammer et al. (2017), Table 6, page 12

or nonexistent. The violence reduction persisted, up to 2 years (when the evaluation ended) (Hammer, 2020).

Place network investigations do not focus on arresting offenders, but it is difficult to disentangle offenders from the places they use. Felony and misdemeanor arrests did not change much in the 24 months after PNI began, compared to the previous 24 months. The changes were not statistically significant usually, suggesting that most changes in arrests may have been random. In PNI site one, however, felony arrests dropped 61%, and misdemeanor arrests went down 35%. In another site, misdemeanor arrests increased significantly (up 39%), but felony arrests showed no significant change. Across all sites, both types of arrests declined (10% for felonies and almost 3% for misdemeanors) (Hammer, 2020, pp. 187–188).

Hammer not only received his doctorate, but the department also promoted him to the rank of captain. The Cincinnati Police Department expanded place network investigations. The Las Vegas police tested a place network investigation strategy at a pilot site. The Las Vegas site experienced a 40 percent reduction in gun violence within the first year (Herold et al., 2020; Herold & Prosser, 2020). More rigorous evaluations are in progress. The strategy has been adopted in cities across the USA, including Dallas, Texas; Denver, Colorado; Philadelphia, Pennsylvania; Tucson, Arizona; and Wichita, Kansas. Several other major cities are exploring place network investigations. Ongoing and future evaluations will help assess the strategy's crime reduction sustainability and determine the circumstances that promote its effectiveness.

Conclusions

Examining the connections among places helps us understand how places create crime within their bounds and within their surroundings. But crime sites can be the tip of a submerged network. In persistent crime hot spots, crime sites may link to hidden crime-involved places. These networks help make violence sticky. It is reasonable to suspect that neighborhoods with more and larger place network infrastructures will have more crime than neighborhoods with few or no such networks. Tamara and Captain Herold speculate that crime place networks arise in locations with conditions that allow crime to flourish (e.g., near transportation access, in areas where low rents encourage poor place management), but we need more information on these environments.

Crime place networks are beyond the capability of local residents to curb through informal social control. Nevertheless, the Cincinnati experience shows the value of including community members on teams designed to uproot crime place networks. The Cincinnati Police place network investigation efforts produced drops in violence but made relatively few arrests. The reductions in violence were almost all due to changing the places that facilitated violence. These efforts not only reduce harms to residents (the many non-offenders and the few offenders), but they also reduce police officers' exposure to risky circumstances. By acknowledging the role and importance of all crime places, we can devise innovative and more effective crime reduction strategies that lessen reliance on standard justice system processes.

Understanding bad networks appears to be very useful. But not everything about place networks has to be doom and gloom. In the next chapter, we look at the utility of understanding good place networks. We show how real estate investors and developers can spread safety throughout an area.

References

Abt, T. (2019). *Bleeding out: The devastating consequences of urban violence - and a bold new plan for peace in the streets*. Basic Books.

Bichler, G., Malm, A., & Enriquez, J. (2014). Magnetic facilities: Identifying the convergence settings of juvenile delinquents. *Crime & Delinquency, 60*(7), 971–998.

Felson, M. (2003). The process of co-offending. In M. J. Smith & D. B. Cornish (Eds.), *Theory for practice in situational crime prevention* (pp. 149–168). Criminal Justice Press.

Hammer, M. (2011). *Crime places of comfort*. Unpublished M.S. demonstration project paper, University of Cincinnati, School of Criminal Justice.

Hammer, M. (2020). *Place-based investigations of violent offender territories (PIVOT): An exploration and evaluation of a place network disruption violence reduction strategy in Cincinnati, Ohio*. Doctoral dissertation, University of Cincinnati.

Hammer, M., Christenson, B., & Madensen, T. D. (2017). *PIVOT: Place-based investigations of violent offender territories*. Herman Goldstein Award submission. June. Cincinnati Police Department. https://popcenter.asu.edu/sites/default/files/17-15.pdf. Accessed 2 Sept 2022.

Herold, T. D., & Eck, J. E. (2020). Gun violence in Cincinnati, Ohio. In M. S. Scott & R. V. Clarke (Eds.), *Problem-oriented policing: Successful case studies* (pp. 28–39). Routledge.

Herold, T. D., Engel, R. S., Corsaro, N., & Clouse, S. L. (2020). *Place network investigations in Las Vegas, Nevada: Program review and process evaluation*. University of Cincinnati, Center for Police Research and Policy.

Herold, T. D., & Prosser, J. (2020). Crime place networks in Las Vegas: A new violence reduction strategy. *Police Chief Magazine, 87*(6), 51–57.

Linning, S. J., & Eck, J. E. (2021). *Whose "eyes on the street" control crime?* Cambridge University Press.

Madensen, T. D., & Eck, J. E. (2013). Crime places and place management. In F. T. Cullen & P. Wilcox (Eds.), *The Oxford handbook of criminological theory* (pp. 554–578). Oxford University Press.

Madensen, T. D., Herold, M., Hammer, M. G., & Christenson, B. R. (2017). Research in brief: Place-based investigations to disrupt crime place networks. *Police Chief Magazine, 84*(4), 14–15.

Chapter 8
The Extended Place Manager III: Place Networks for Safety

In the last two chapters, we looked at the blade of the crime hockey stick: the high-crime places making trouble for places nearby. In this chapter, we look at the handle: low-crime places that radiate safety. Crime researchers have not investigated this topic, with the exception of one of us. So, we will rely mostly on Shannon's field work in Cincinnati. Her work draws from the works of architectural journalist Jane Jacobs. Jacobs was the first person to discuss how place managers exert and expand their control to create safety. Two of us have published a detailed account of Jacobs' ideas and their applicability to criminology (Linning & Eck, 2021).

In the first sections, we cover two of Jacobs' (1961) ideas—*eyes on the street* and the *constant succession of eyes*—to show how place managers can spread safety beyond their places' boundaries. We then describe how place managers expand their control through networks.

Jane Jacobs' *Eyes on the Street*

Jane Jacobs shook the urban planning field with her debut book, *The Death and Life of Great American Cities* (1961). She provided a sharp critique of entrenched city planning theory. Initially, her book polarized the field. With time, her new ideas have become entrenched within urban planning (Kanigel, 2016; Page, 2011).

For those narrowly concerned about crime, her most notable contribution was coining the phrase *eyes on the street*. These eyes belong those who exert surveillance over urban areas. To Jacobs, urban areas are safer when we design urban environments to facilitate street watching.

Criminologists usually claim that the eyes belong to *residents*. They assume Jacobs claimed residents were keeping order on the street. But our examination of her work—looking at each of her examples, studying her explanations, and reading articles and books Jacobs wrote before and after her most famous book—shows that she was referring to mostly shopkeepers, business owners, and other place managers and seldom residents (Linning & Eck, 2021).

Jacobs (1961; p. 34) argued that the eyes on the street "[belong] to those we might call the natural proprietors of the street." Shopkeepers and business owners made up most of her examples illustrating nongovernment agents who intervene effectively in sidewalk activity. She pointed out that shopkeepers have strong economic incentives to guard their properties. Creating safe places increases the likelihood that more people will patronize their shops. So these shopkeepers keep close guard of their places:

> …storekeepers and other small businessmen are typically strong proponents of peace and order themselves; they hate broken windows and holdups; they had having customers made nervous about safety. They are great street watchers and sidewalk guardians if present in sufficient numbers. (Jacobs, 1961, p. 37)

Jacobs foreshadowed place management theory 30 years before John created it without knowing what Jacobs said (Eck, 1994). The actions of shopkeepers form the core of her ideas on safety. Place managers are the people who make their places safe. But Jacobs also described how shopkeepers create safety along streets: their linear purlieus. Street blocks can be kept safe by a *constant succession of eyes* (Jacobs, 1961, p. 50). What did she mean by "constant succession?"

Jane Jacobs' *Constant Succession of Eyes*

Criminologists citing Jacobs often discuss how she pushed for mixed land use to increase eyes on the street. Mixed land use to criminologists is an area with both residential and commercial property. But Jacobs had a more expansive understanding of what it means for an area to be mixed. She meant a mix of types of businesses and shops. A street segment with a bar, a couple of restaurants, a grocery, a clothing shop, apartments, a hardware store, a nail solon, and a host of other businesses is mixed. A street with only restaurants and apartments is not. Streets containing diverse businesses create an "intricacy of sidewalk use, bringing with it a constant succession of eyes" that increases guardianship widely (p. 50). Ideally, there should be eyes on the street nearly all hours of the day.

Jacobs argued that the safest streets had a mixture of businesses, collectively open nearly all hours of the day. Jacobs spent a great deal of time observing streets. Beginning in the morning, she saw storeowners opening their shops: like bakeries, laundromats, and delicatessens. These place managers watched of the street. By the end of the workday, as some businesses shuttered their doors and windows, others—like pubs, theaters, and restaurants—opened. In many cases, they remained open well after midnight (Jacobs, 1961; Linning & Eck, 2021). Having early and late opening businesses on the same segment creates Jacobs' constant succession of eyes to watch over the street.

Figure 8.1 illustrates the constant succession of eyes. At the top of Fig. 8.1, we show the location of shops along three hypothetical street segments. The bottom portion of the figure shows the hours place managers are active at these places. Some businesses—such as bakeries, coffee shops, and gyms—tend to open earlier. Other places—such as banks and offices—are open during standard work hours. Other businesses—such as movie theaters, bars, and clubs—tend to be open later.

We pause here to note that we do not describe what is going on above street level: buildings may contain apartments or condominium units, or office space for small firms (marketing consultant, law firm, dentist office, web developer, karate studio, and so on), or even co-working space. These activities may also contribute to the succession of eyes. Nevertheless, the street-level perspective is sufficient to tell our story.

If we want a constant succession of eyes, we do not want to cluster places with similar hours of operation. Take banks and office buildings as an example. They typically hold midday business hours, often 9 am to 5 pm. Segments consisting only of those types of places will have no eyes on those segments from 5 pm until 9 am. Instead, placing them on adjacent blocks staggers them across several street segments. The same goes for restaurants. Many are open similar hours so staggering them across segments, albeit still close by, is desirable.

Ideally, we want a mixture of early, midday, and late opening places on the same street segment. For example, while a bakery may open at 6 am, bakers must arrive earlier to have their baked goods ready for opening. This means place managers are stationed at the property as early as 4 am. Similarly, employees of gyms arrive for openings as early as 5 am. We do not need to station the gym on the same segment as the bakery because that street segment already has eyes stationed at the bakery. It would be wise to situate the gym down the street. Then that block has eyes early in the morning too. We can also sprinkle some coffee shops—which often open

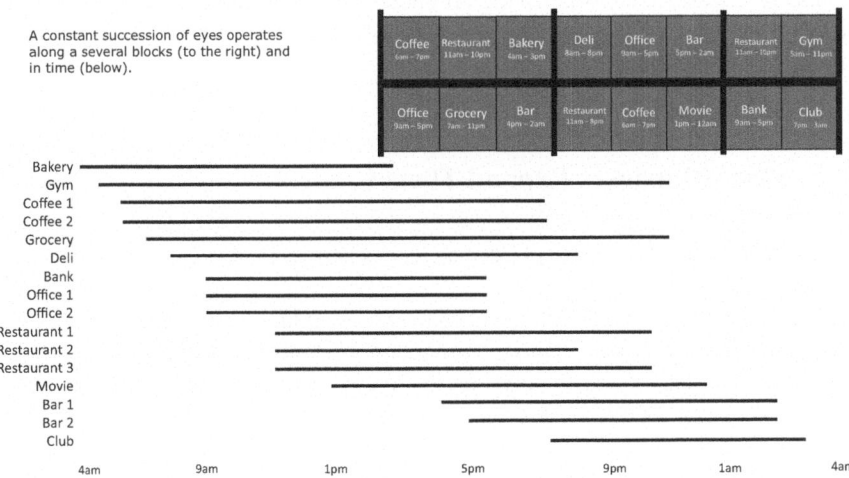

Fig. 8.1 Constant succession of eyes

between 5 am and 8 am—to create overlapping eyes between the bakery and the gym. A diner, which serves breakfast and lunch, also would add to the succession of eyes. We then fill in the gaps with midday places—like banks and offices—and late-night places, such as theaters, bars, and clubs.

Total heterogeneity is not required, however. It is fine to have two offices on the same block. What's most important is that they are accompanied by other places with staggered business hours, such as a gym, restaurant, and bar. What is important is whether there is a sufficient coverage of eyes on the street for as many hours as possible.

Not only does creating a constant succession of eyes have potential crime control benefits, but it can also have economic rewards. Many business owners benefit from having complementary businesses near them. Bars and pubs, for example, can profit from being close to restaurants. While waiting for one's dinner reservation, some customers might stop in at a nearby bar for a drink. A more deliberate example would be pub-crawls. When bars cluster, they can organize such events through social media to attract more customers. Economists refer to this phenomenon as agglomeration economies (Glaeser, 2010). It's the idea that clustering similar places together brings more economic benefit. But agglomerating all businesses of the same type on a street segment is not good for safety. If they are staggered, with diverse businesses in-between, agglomeration benefits can be achieved while creating Jacobs' constant succession of eyes.

It may seem daunting to apply Jacobs' concept of succession to cities. How could we possibly coordinate the position of different types of places? Though city planning departments can have influence, much of it must come from property developers who own much of a city's places. Research has revealed that owning multiple properties to control the characteristics of larger areas is a deliberate business tactic used by place managers (Linning, 2019). They create networks of places to extend their control of city areas and generate more profits. They also get to decide who leases their storefronts. So understanding their decision-making processes is important. We turn to the tactics owners use to extend control beyond the boundaries of their places next.

How Place Managers Expand Their Control

Figure 8.2 shows four ways place managers exert control. Let us look at each method in detail.

First, a person can exert safety and control over a place by purchasing it. As discussed in Chap. 3, owners organize their space. They also control access and regulate conduct of place users. Finally, they engage in activities to acquire resources so that the place can continue to function.

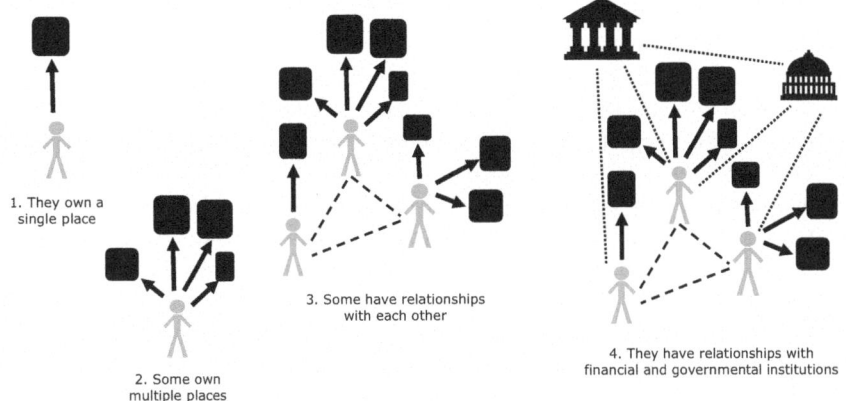

Fig. 8.2 How place managers extend their control. (Adapted from Linning & Eck, 2021, p. 45)

Second, if a place manager can purchase additional properties. Ownership of places is concentrated just as crime is concentrated: a relatively few owners control a large proportion of properties in a city (Eck, 2019; Payne, 2010). Ownership creates a network of places owned by the same person or company.

This is a commonly used tactic by developers. One Cincinnati developer explained to Shannon that he would purchase several buildings in transitioning neighborhoods. When the first building was redeveloped, he invited prospective tenants to tour its units. To allay their anxiety about living in a neighborhood with crime problems, he pointed to the other buildings he owned and told the prospective tenant he is redeveloping them just like the one they are in now. He had control over the street block and they would be part of the area's renaissance if they came while rents were low. The developer claimed this tactic convinced many apprehensive applicants to sign leases. Our observations of the area suggest he was telling the truth (Linning & Eck, 2021).

Other developers use this tactic to eliminate problems that neighboring properties may create. In another example from Shannon's research, a developer was concerned about a payday lending business in the area where he owned properties. He believed the business was contributing to the neighborhood's unsavory reputation and feared its presence dissuaded people from renting units and patronizing the stores he owned. So he found the owner of the property and purchased it. Once he owned the building, he informed the payday lender that he would not renew the business' lease when it expired. He then redeveloped the building and leased it to small business owners.

These networks of places provide a great deal of control to owners. But place managers can extend their control even further when they create partnerships with other place managers. This is the third way place managers can expand control.

Several place managers have described the benefits of these partnerships in both development and business management.

Developers often do not work alone. One developer told Shannon of how he created an urban village with some of his business partners. They spent years purchasing properties in a neighborhood and working to create a family-friendly shopping and entertainment area that attracted people from outside the area. However, a vacant property nearby was a problem. The building held several squatters who used illicit drugs and engaged in other illegal activities. These activities, the developers believed, would make the people they wanted to attract feel unsafe and less likely to come to the area. After they discussed the matter, one of the developers purchased the property and renovated the building. He then rented the apartments above street level and leased the refurbished storefront units to small business owners.

Some business owners lease their site, rather than own the property. They too use networks to radiate safety. Shannon interviewed the manager of a coffee shop who shared her outdoor patio space with a neighboring restaurant. The owners of the two businesses worked together to watch over each other's properties and the shared space. The owner described how the two businesses created a succession of eyes. The coffee shop's employees arrived at 6 am to open the shop at 6:30. They served as *eyes* for both businesses until the restaurant's employees arrived at 10:30 am. The coffee shop closed at 6:30 pm and its employees left by 7. The restaurant's employees stayed until 10:30 pm. Instead of each business guarding its property for around 12 hours per day, the two businesses coordinated guardianship for nearly 17 hours daily. To our knowledge, neither business owner had read Jane Jacobs' book, but they were putting her ideas into practice.

These are small-scale examples of place managers working together. You can see larger examples with business improvement districts (BIDs). BIDs are areas where all businesses within them agree to pay an additional tax. The BID uses the tax revenues to fund projects within its boundaries, including the deployment of *ambassadors* in distinctive jackets (Hoyt, 2004; Manshel, 2020). BIDs can be quite powerful; they can apply pressure on place managers within their territory to curtail troublesome activities. For example, BID members applied informal pressure on the manager of a convenience store near an elementary school to curb sales of single cans of inexpensive refrigerated beer. If the place manager did not comply, the BID threatened to take matters to the city (these discussions were friendly, private, and unrecorded).

Fourth, place managers can link to financial and governmental institutions. In areas rife with dilapidated buildings, governments may create financial incentives for property developers to invest in real estate. Governments may also offer tax abatements to developers who purchase and redevelop properties in deteriorating areas (Peters & Fisher, 2004). Shannon interviewed a city manager who recounted that several large corporations threatened to leave a city, taking many of their employees with them, if the city did not increase investment to revitalize the downtown core. This was a sufficient motivator for the city to spearhead that process.

Extending safety

This city public park is operated by the area's redevelopment organization.

However, the reverse is also true. Although place managers have a great deal of control over their properties, there are limits to their powers. Governments and financial institutions can influence place managers' decisions through means like regulation and civil litigation. As discussed in Chap. 5, super controllers are best equipped to apply these incentives (Sampson et al., 2010). To run a bar, for example, the place manager must obtain a liquor license. If a place manager fails to abide by the regulations set out in the license, a liquor board agent can revoke the license, which prevents the bar from operating. The threat of losing one's liquor license is a strong economic motivator to get the place manager of the bar to change his business operations. In another example, we witnessed a BID requesting the local government to step up enforcement against a liquor retailer because of the disorder in and around the business.

Financial institutions can also influence place management decisions. One developer recounted a decades-old story to Shannon about the difficulty purchasing several properties because banks had redlined the area. Redlining was a common practice, beginning in the 1930s, when the US government's Federal Housing Administration (FHA) began. Because of FHA incentives, financial institutions denied mortgages to anyone requesting a loan to purchase property in redlined areas. Bank redlining decisions were largely driven in part by the racial composition of neighborhoods, and its impacts persist to present day (Rothstein, 2017). It has also influenced crime patterns (Linning & Eck, 2021; Linning et al., 2022). The developer explained to Shannon that he would have purchased property in the area, but because the banks refused to finance the purchases, it caused him to pursue property investment elsewhere. In this example, financial institutions starved good place management.

But financial institutions can also support place management. The Cincinnati Center City Development Corporation (commonly referred to as 3CDC) is a nonprofit developer established by a public-private partnership including city government and large local corporations. Using a combination of conventional bank loans, tax incentives, and funding from corporations, 3CDC transformed an extremely high-crime area of Cincinnati, with few businesses, into a low-crime thriving residential, commercial, entertainment area. It buys, develops, and sells property and it helps businesses that want to move into the area. Although its mandate covers many square blocks, it is 3CDC's funding of development of individual buildings and lots that created the change (Demeropolis & Wetterich, 2019; Smith, 2015; Woodard, 2016).

Implications

What does this all mean for crime control? All four sources of control show that control starts at places and extends to larger areas (Linning et al., 2022). Once place managers create safe places, these places attract more people to the area. The additional people make street segments more attractive to new businesses. And these new businesses add eyes on the street. Note that we follow closely to Jacobs' description: it is the businesses that put eyes on the street. The residents, pedestrians, and car occupants are not the primary source of the eyes (Linning & Eck, 2021).

Place managers have several mechanisms for enhancing safety beyond their individual places. We noted the development of a constant succession of eyes created by the variable opening times of businesses on a block. A constant succession of eyes might develop naturally, but we suspect such a development will be rare and unstable. Coordination is more likely to create stable constant eye succession. How can coordination occur? First, some place owners own many places. A developer can choose street-level tenants in ways to create succession of eyes (Linning, 2019). Second, place managers create networks. Sometimes these are informal arrangements. Sometimes these are formal; business improvement districts are an example of a very formal arrangement. Third, place managers have connections to government agencies and financial institutions. These agencies and institutions can facilitate coordination by connecting place managers who might not otherwise come into contact.

The radiation of safety suggests why some neighborhoods have less crime than others. In areas where place managers radiate safety, there will be less crime. In areas where they do not, there will be more crime. Linning and Eck (2021) call this emphasis on place management a neo-Jacobian perspective, to acknowledge Jane Jacobs' emphasis on the importance of shopkeepers in keeping streets safe. The neo-Jacobian perspective sees a much smaller role to residents in creating safety. Jacobs, in her discussions of neighborhoods, downplayed the role of residents as a social force. Instead, she emphasized the role of residents as a political force (Jacobs, 1961). Residents can demand greater government services, call for the removal of crime-prone places, obstruct the development of places that may disrupt their lives, work with place managers, and many other things. But daily informal collective action to produce safety is not as powerful as the role of place managers. This is particularly true when residents do not own places and consequently have limited powers over how places are managed.

Residents can demand that local governments do a better job at regulating places so that they promote safety. In the next chapter, we look at regulation and other ways to prevent crime at places.

References

Demeropolis, T., & Wetterich, C. (2019, March 21). How (and why) 3CDC works. *Cincinnati Business Courier.* https://www.bizjournals.com/cincinnati/news/2019/03/15/how-and-why-3cdc-works.html. Accessed 12 Mar 2019.

Eck, J. E. (1994). *Drug markets and drug places: A case-control study of the spatial structure of illicit drug dealing* (Unpublished doctoral dissertation). University of Maryland College Park.

Eck, J. E. (2019). Race, place management, and crime. In J. D. Unnever, S. L. Gabbidon, & C. Chouhy (Eds.), *Building a black criminology: Race, theory, and crime* (pp. 171–206). Routledge.

Glaeser, E. L. (2010). Introduction. In E. L. Glaeser (Ed.), *Agglomeration economics* (pp. 1–12). University of Chicago Press.

Hoyt, L. (2004). Collecting private funds for safer public spaces: An empirical examination of the business improvement district concept. *Environment and Planning B: Planning and Design, 31*(3), 367–380.

Jacobs, J. (1961). *The death and life of great American cities.* Vintage.

Kanigel, R. (2016). *Eyes on the street: The life of Jane Jacobs.* Penguin Random House.

Linning, S. J. (2019). *The Neo-Jacobian perspective of place and neighborhood crime: A case study of property management, redevelopment, and crime in Walnut Hills, Cincinnati, Ohio* (Unpublished doctoral dissertation). University of Cincinnati.

Linning, S. J., & Eck, J. E. (2021). *Whose "eyes on the street" control crime? Expanding place management into neighborhoods.* Cambridge University Press.

Linning, S. J., Olaghere, A., & Eck, J. E. (2022). Say NOPE to social disorganization criminology: The importance of creators in neighborhood social control. *Crime Science, 11*(5), 1–11.

Manshel, A. (2020). *Learning from Bryant Park: Revitalizing cities, towns, and public spaces.* Rutgers University Press.

Page, M. (2011). Introduction: More than meets the eye. In M. Page & T. Mennel (Eds.), *Reconsidering Jane Jacobs* (pp. 3–14). American Planning Association.

Payne, T. C. (2010). *Does changing ownership change crime? An analysis of apartment ownership and crime in Cincinnati* (Unpublished Doctoral Dissertation). University of Cincinnati.

Peters, A., & Fisher, P. (2004). The failures of economic development incentives. *Journal of the American Planning Association, 70*(1), 27–37.

Rothstein, R. (2017). *The color of law: A forgotten history of how our government segregated America.* Liveright.

Sampson, R., Eck, J. E., & Dunham, J. (2010). Super controllers and crime prevention: A routine activity explanation of crime prevention success and failure. *Security Journal, 23*(1), 37–51.

Smith, R. J. (2015, October 5). 3CDC in over-the-Rhine: Between two worlds. *Cincinnati Magazine.* http://www.cincinnatimagazine.com/citywiseblog/3cdc-in-over-the-rhine-between-two-worlds/. Accessed 20 Oct 2020.

Woodard, C. (2016, June 16). How Cincinnati salvaged the nation's most dangerous neighborhood: Leaning on the power of local corporations, officials engineered an renaissance in the city's heart. *Politico.* https://www.politico.com/magazine/story/2016/06/what-works-cincinnati-ohio-over-the-rhine-crime-neighborhood-turnaround-city-urban-revitalization-213969/. Accessed Aug.

Chapter 9
Reducing Crime at High-Crime Places

It is easier to keep high-crime places in check when many places radiate safety. Still, we would be naïve if we put all our faith in the private place market to fight crime, particularly in areas with established crime places. So in this chapter, we examine three approaches local governments can use to tackle crime.

The first approach is police hot spots patrols. These are a popular way to tackle crime concentrations. Many studies show that these patrols can reduce crime, at least temporarily. Nevertheless, hot spots patrols are not good foundational strategy when place managers are at the core of the problem.

Problem-oriented policing, the second approach, is far superior to hot spots patrols, and the evidence supports this claim. However, problem-oriented policing relies on cooperation between police and place managers. Cooperation is often possible, but when place managers fain cooperation and resist meaningful changes, problem-oriented policing bogs down.

The third approach calls for local governments to regulate places. We examine two ways they can do this; one way has broad applicability, and the other should be reserved for special circumstances. We close this chapter with a comprehensive strategy using all three approaches regulation its foundation.

The Limits of Hot Spots Patrols

When police leaders ask for evidence-based crime control tactics, hot spots policing is at the top of the list. Anthony Braga and colleagues have produced four systematic reviews of the many evaluations of hot spots patrols. The latest (Braga et al., 2019) examined 73 findings (from 62 studies), including 35 findings from randomized controlled studies. Like its predecessors (Braga et al., 2014; Braga, 2001, 2005), the latest review found that hot spots patrols can reduce violence, property crimes, disorder, and drug offenses (Braga et al., 2019).

As we noted in Chap. 7, the precise meaning of the term *hot spot* varies from experiment to experiment (Ratcliffe, 2014; Weisburd & Telep, 2014). A geographic crime concentration can be as small as an address or as large as multiple city blocks. In the paper describing the first hot spots experiment, Lawrence Sherman and David Weisburd (1995: p. 630) defined a hot spot as "...as small clusters of addresses with frequent 'hard' crime calls as well as substantial 'soft' crime calls for service ... We then limited the boundaries of each spot conceptually as easily visible from an epicenter...." Other experiments defined hot spots as addresses (Hope, 1994; Sherman & Rogan, 1995a). Even more researchers define a hot spot as a small group of connected street segments and intersections (Braga et al., 1999; Weisburd & Green, 1995). Some researchers let their mapping algorithms define compact areas (Ratcliffe et al., 2011; Rosenfeld et al., 2014). And some researchers even use census block groupings (Santos & Santos, 2016). The term *hot spot* is so vague that researchers sometimes use it to describe areas even larger than census blocks (e.g., Sherman & Rogan, 1995b). Given the range of areas researchers call hot spots, it is quite likely that most hot spots patrols are covering purlieus and are not pinpointing the source of the problem.

Just as the definition of a hot spot is imprecise, so are the interventions police apply. Sherman and Weisburd (1995) examined the presence of police in vehicles at hot spots. Their experiment studied Minneapolis patrol officers going to hot spots, sitting in their cars, and then leaving. Other hot spots experiments have had officers wander around on foot (Ratcliffe et al., 2011). In 2008, a survey of police agencies found a wide array of tactics applied (PERF, 2008).

Anthony Braga and coauthors (2019) divided police actions at hot spots into two categories: those that try to deter possible offenders by police presence or aggressive tactics and those that try to block crime opportunities through forms of problem-solving. We will talk more about problem-solving in the next sections. For now, problem-solving tactics involve police trying to determine why the spot is hot and identifying what can be done to change these conditions. When Braga and coauthors (2019) compared aggressive hot spot policing to problem-solving hot spot policing, they found that problem-solving was more effective at driving down crime and disorder than aggressive tactics.

Critics allege that hot spots policing drives down crime in the hot spot by shoving it to a nearby formerly cold or cool spot. If so, little is gained. Although such pessimism is common, as we showed in Chap. 6, it is wrong. There has been a great deal of research on crime displacement and several systematic reviews of the evidence for displacement (Barr & Pease, 1990; Eck, 1993; Hesseling, 1994; Guerette & Bowers, 2009; Bowers et al., 2011). The most recent and most comprehensive review found that displacement is far from inevitable (Bowers et al., 2011). In fact, most evaluations show no evidence of crime displacement. When evaluations find displacement, the displacement effect is less than the total crime reduction. That is, the interventions eliminate more crimes than they displace.

Perhaps more shocking to the pessimists is the well-documented fact, discussed in Chap. 6, that safety displaces. Ronald V. Clarke and David Weisburd (1994) called these positive phenomena the diffusion of crime control benefits: the opposite of displacement. A diffusion effect is present when the police intervene at a hot spot, drive crime down at the spot, and drive down crime in the untreated areas near the hot spot. The evidence shows that the diffusion of benefits is at least as common as displacement (Bowers et al., 2011; Guerette & Bowers, 2009).

Despite the considerable evidence, there are four drawbacks to hot spots patrols. First, there is no consistency in the use of the term *hot spot*. Rarely are police focused on proprietary places. They are patrolling an area around a hot place, perhaps. If the crimes that drew police attention are inside, roaming the streets may have little effect. If a proprietary place is radiating crime into its purlieu, patrols may suppress purlieu crimes while leaving the source of the problem unaddressed. If crime places are networked, as we described in Chap. 7, patrols can be a useful palliative, but once the patrols move to another hot spot, the crimes will return.

This brings us to the second difficulty. When police commanders tell their officers to sit in a hot spot and do not direct them to look into why a hot spot has crime and do something about it, these patrols have weak effects. Problem-solving tactics may be more powerful than deterrence and arrests because problem-solving may penetrate places when patrolling cannot. There are reasons offenders are at a hot spot, and if the police do not address these reasons, the crime will reappear after the patrolling declines.

This wear-off in effectiveness is the third drawback to hot spots patrols. Lawrence Sherman's (1990) theory of police hot spots patrols assumed crime would return. When Sherman developed his theory, the idea that one could change place management practices to reduce hot spot crime had not appeared. A third of a century later, we know better.

Finally, hot spots patrols can drive up arrest rates. Arrests are costly, not just to offenders, but to the taxpaying public. If there were no alternative ways to reduce crime, this might be acceptable. But there are good alternatives.

The Advantages of Problem-Oriented Policing

Problem-oriented policing directs police to solve problems, whether crime related or other types. Police operating in a problem-oriented manner identify patterns of harmful events. They then dig into the problem to discover why the problem is occurring at precise places, definite times, and to particular people, rather than at other places, other times, and to other people. This analysis often leads to the discovery of key features of the problem. Altering these can lead to the problem's collapse (Goldstein, 1979). When crime or disorder concentrates at proprietary places, the key features are usually under the control of place managers.

Within a problem-oriented approach, police are encouraged to seek out a wide variety of possible solutions, including solutions that do not rely upon the police. In fact, it is desirable to shift the burden of addressing a problem from the shoulder of the police (and taxpayers) and onto the shoulders of the people and organizations that create problem-facilitating conditions: as long as shifting solves the problem (Scott, 2004). This is why police try to work with managers to alter places.

Police are left to handle crime places

A police sergeant working on a place problem, around 2005. Since her work, the city has increased its regulation of crime-involved places.

There have been many evaluations of police problem-solving. Two systematic reviews and meta-analyses of these studies demonstrate that problem-oriented policing is an effective approach (Weisburd et al., 2010; Hinkle et al., 2020). One study compared problem-solving at drug dealing hot spots to hot spots enforcement. The study found that problem-solving worked better (Weisburd & Green, 1995). We noted earlier that the effectiveness of hot spot policing programs using problem solving is greater than such patrols using aggressive tactics (Braga et al., 2014, 2015, 2019).

Much of what we know about proprietary places comes from problem-solving projects (Eck, 2015), including the central role of place managers (Eck, 1994). Problem-solving led to the place network investigations program described in Chap. 7. Malcolm Sparrow, a leading expert on regulation, has developed a comprehensive theory of regulation based on problem-oriented policing (Sparrow, 2000, 2008). And unique among policing strategies, researchers and practitioners have developed and published a wide variety of manuals and guides to assist police, community members, and place managers address problems (Center for Problem-Oriented Policing, 2022).

There are two limits to the usefulness to a problem-oriented approach. First, it requires analytical skills and experience possessed by relatively few people, within and outside of policing. Police and their publics reflexively adopt solutions to problems they know little about. Often problem-solving efforts develop after the police have failed with their standard approaches. Still, police can accomplish much with a small team of problem-solvers who have the necessary skills.

Second, solutions to chronic problems often require public and private organizations to take actions they prefer not to. Place managers may find the solutions are costly or disruptive, at least in the short run. The police have very limited authority to compel place managers to take the appropriate action (Buerger, 1994). And getting that authority can be costly.

Problem-solving may be more effective when conducted as part of a regulatory process. Regulation may provide incentives for place managers to attend to budding problems, acting before the problem grows large enough to require police attention. Regulation can give place managers incentives to work with police and nearby place managers. A regulatory context to problem-solving prevents place managers from ignoring solutions that could reduce crime at their places. However, the form of regulation matters.

The Centrality of Regulation

Rather than take on high-crime places one at a time, a regulatory approach takes on types of places, sometimes before they become problems. In 2012, John co-wrote an article with his daughter describing a range of regulatory approaches to reducing crime at places (Eck & Eck, 2012; Eck, 2018). They distinguished between two categories of regulation: means focused and ends focused.

Regulating the Means for Reducing Crime

When people think of regulation, they usually think of means-focused regulation. This type regulation prescribes solutions—rules and procedures to follow, technology to use, or information to record—and holds place managers accountable for following rules, using technology, and recording information. Prescriptions are useful when we have strong evidence the solutions work well in most settings. And means-focused regulation may be the only alternative when a crime is so serious we cannot tolerate even one event. Security at airports to prevent aircraft hijacking is of this type.

There are two types of means-focused regulation:

- *Command and Control*—The regulator tells the place manager what to do to reduce crime. Mandating specific crime prevention technology (e.g., lighting, cameras, fencing, or locks) is an example. When regulatory agencies inspect bars and pubs, they examine the procedures used by bar staff, whether they have received the required training, and how they check identification to prevent serving minors. These are means for preventing misuse of alcohol, drunk driving, and

related offenses. All bars must use the same means, even if they have no history of alcohol-related problems.
- *Subsidizing*—The regulator provides the technology or training that the place manager would otherwise have to purchase from a private vendor. For example, many police agencies provide free landlord training programs to help rental property owners keep crime down (Campbell, 2000). Alternatively, the regulator can reimburse investments in technology or give a tax break for implementing a crime prevention technology. Usually subsidies to engage in prevention are available to high- and low-crime places.

Whether commanding or subsidizing, demanding that place managers use particular means makes little sense if we do not have strong evidence that these means usually work. Sadly, strong evidence is often lacking. A command without evidence risks wasting the place manager's resources on actions of no use to the public. A subsidy for prevention that does not take a bite out of crime wastes the taxpayer's money. The risks of acting without evidence may be worth it when the crimes we need to suppress are extraordinarily serious—like terrorist bombings or school shootings. The government agency needs to act now, and experimentation takes time or is impossible. Even then, we would want the agency to generate evidence so future prevention efforts can be made to be less expensive, more effective, and less burdensome.

Regulating the Ends of Crime Prevention

Ends-focused regulation does not prescribe solutions. It is up to the place manager to find the solution that best fits her situation. Instead, ends-focused regulation sets limits to the level of crime or disorder. For example, if a city has 100 bars and 800 bar fights reported to the police, then an ends-focused approach might cap the number of fights at any bar at four per year. Bar owners can organize their space, regulate patron conduct, and control drinkers' access to make sure they do not exceed that limit. If no bar exceeds the four-fight limit, then the city would have cut bar fights in half without dictating how each bar should operate.

There are three ends-focused regulatory approaches:

- *Civil litigation*—Suing owners of properties with high levels of crime (particularly violent crime) may provide an incentive for property owners to attend to crime prevention. However, this depends on who brings the suit. There is no evidence that private suits, usually following a heinous crime, prevent crime. Here the victim (or the victim's estate, if she is dead) brings the suit, alleging that the operators of the place are responsible for the crime. In principle, the threat of such suits could induce place managers to invest in prevention. However, private attorneys, paid only if they win a case against a large company, may be reluctant to sue place managers without resources, even if they operate high-crime locations. Instead, private attorneys may focus their attention on relatively safe places owned by corporations with deep pockets (Eck, 1997). More promising are suits by local governments against owners of high-crime places. These plaintiffs seek a change in the operation of the place, or its closing, rather than compensation. Evidence reveals that threats of these suits reduce crime (Mazerolle & Ransley, 2005; Worrall & Wheeler, 2019).

- *Capping crime or disorder*—The regulator can put ceiling on the number of calls to police that can originate from a place. Those many places in the hockey stick's handle never approach the limit. Owners of the places in the stick's blade must find ways not to exceed the limit. Caps on false alarms are an example of this type of regulation. After a place reaches the cap, police charge the place owner the costs of the response, issue a fine, or do not respond. Some cities put a limit on police calls from rental property (Payne, 2016), but exempt from the limit domestic violence and other calls where there is a fear of suppressing the need for police attention (Desmond & Valdez, 2012). The City of Chula Vista threatens motel owners with business license revocation if their places exceed a cap on calls to the police (Bichler et al., 2013).
- *Tradable permits*—Instead of establishing a per place cap, the regulator sets a cap on the total number of regulated crime or disorder events. It then issues permits to places for a limited number of events. The total number of permits issued is substantially below typical crime levels. Thus, if all permits are used, crime still goes down. Permit holders can buy and sell unused permits. Remember the example of the 100 bars caped at four fights per year? In a tradeable permit regime, a bar owner could sell her permits to other bar owners. She earns money for running a safe place, the other bar owners have to pay more for not running safe places, and the police handle fewer fights. We have not heard of a government using tradable permits to reduce crime, but environmental regulators have a history of success with tradable permits to curtail pollution (Ellerman, 2006).

Table 9.1 shows that governments use a variety of regulatory approaches to address a broad spectrum of crime and disorder.

The choice of the type of regulation depends on the characteristics of the crime problem, but three characteristics stand out: crime seriousness, crime volume, and the availability of evidence. The decision tree in Fig. 9.1 shows how a local government can choose whether to use a means- or ends-based regulatory strategy. Most crime is low to moderate in seriousness but high in volume, and usually the evidence backing the use of means is weak or lacking. This is path A, which leads to ends-based regulations. Path B is for extremely serious crimes with low frequency (e.g., school shootings). It leads to ends-based regulation. If the crimes are not serious and are infrequent and there are no evidence-backed solutions, then regulation may not be justified (path C). If crime is low to moderately serious and there are evidence-based solutions, then D paths lead to means-based solutions.

All regulatory approaches to crime shift the responsibility to provide safe and secure places from police and taxpayers to the people responsible for operating the places. When a few places are responsible for much of the crime and disorder, then

Table 9.1 Examples of regulatory instruments to control crime at places

Crime	Place	Regulation	Subtype	References
Means regulated				
Commercial robbery	Convenience stores	Specifying at least two clerks must be on duty at convenience stores at night	Command and control	Clifton Jr. (1987)
Terrorist attacks	Airports	Mandatory security measures, including passenger and baggage screening	Command and control	Frederickson and LaPorte (2002)
Drug dealing	Rental property	Police provide landlords with training	Subsidy	Campbell (2000)
Ends regulated				
Violent crime	Rental housing	Premises liability suits against owners of places where someone was grievously attacked	Civil suits (victim plaintiff)	Kennedy and Hupp (1998)
Drug dealing	Rental property	Nuisance abatement suits	Civil suits (government plaintiff)	Mazerolle and Ransley (2005)
Calls to police	Rental property	Landlords whose property exceeds maximum number of calls to police are fined	Cap and fines	Payne (2016)
False alarms	Places using alarms to call for police	Fines for every alarm over a maximum number	Cap and fines	Sampson (2007)
Calls to police	Motels	Business licenses are revoked for motels that exceed maximum level of calls to police	Cap and close	Bichler et al. (2013)

Table adapted from Eck (2018, p. 113)

the taxpaying owners of the many low-crime places are subsidizing the owners of the few high-crime places.

It is not surprising that when police request changes to the few high-crime places, their place managers resist. They have to change their business models. And these business models frequently depend on the police to provide free security services.

If police requests occurred against a backdrop of regulation, there would be greater incentive for the place managers to work with the police. Against a backdrop of regulation, if nearby safe-place managers ask the crime-place manager to cooperate in lowering crime, it is more likely the manager of the high-crime place will sit down at the table.

But the form of regulation matters. Means-based regulation, based on compliance with generic solutions that might not work in specific conditions, may not encourage problem-solving. High-crime place managers can excuse themselves by saying that they comply with the rules. Ends-based regulation, with its emphasis on

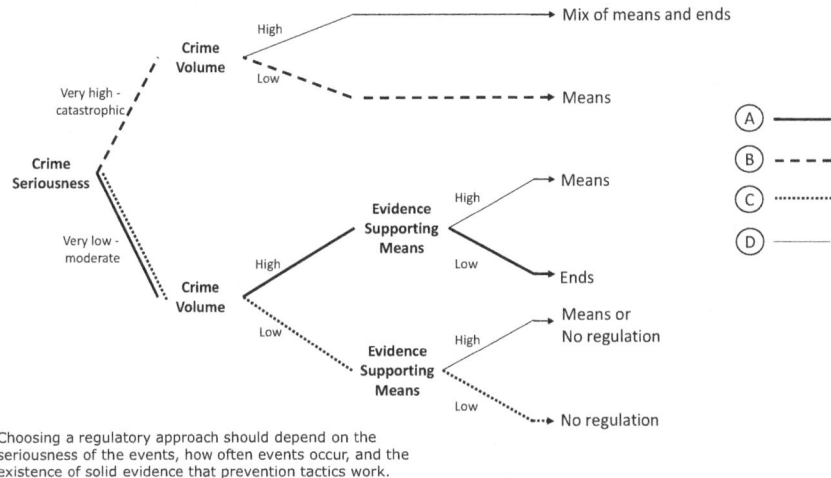

Fig. 9.1 Choosing regulatory approaches for crime places. (Adapted from Eck, 2018)

outcomes and willingness to be flexible about solutions, may be more useful. Now place managers are free to experiment with solutions that fit their particular circumstances and budgets.

Some people assume that holding place managers accountable takes offenders off the hook. Catching offenders is not the subject of this book, so we have not discussed it. Nevertheless, we need to state that regulations are not a substitute for catching offenders; police should pursue offenders as much as they did before regulation. Although there is considerable value to society for catching people who commit crimes, it is a mistake to believe that catching criminals will put a serious dent in crime if place managers continue to facilitate crime by making the life of offenders easy and rewarding. When regulation works, there are fewer crime-facilitating places, so there are far fewer offenses, so there are fewer offenders to catch.

A Comprehensive Place-Based Strategy

Moving forward, policy makers should consider a place-based strategy that makes use of all the approaches we have discussed. Regulation would be the primary approach. Local governments would use ends-focused regulation for common, high-volume, crimes concentrated at proprietary places. For the extremely serious uncommon crimes, governments would use a means-focused approach. Local government would also use problem-oriented policing to address those remaining high-crime places. It would be particularly useful when confronting a network of crime-involved places (Chap. 7). Regulation would provide greater incentives for managers of these places to work with the police to find and adopt meaningful solutions. In a crisis and for short periods, police could use hot spots patrols. However, hot spots policing would not be the foundation of crime control. It would be a temporary bandage to buy time for a problem-solving solution to take hold and for regulators to effect change.

References

Barr, R. & Pease, K. (1990). Crime placement, displacement and deflection. In M. Tonry & N. Morris (Eds.), *Crime and justice: A review of research* (Vol. 12, pp. 277–318). University of Chicago Press.

Bichler, G., Schmerler, K., & Enriquez, J. (2013). Curbing nuisance motels: An evaluation of police as place regulators. *Policing: An International Journal of Police Strategies & Management, 36*(2), 437–462.

Bowers, K. J., Johnson, S. D., Guerette, R. T., Summers, L., & Poynton, S. 2011. Spatial displacement and diffusion of benefits among geographically focused policing initiatives: A meta-analytical review. *Journal of Experimental Criminology, 7*(4), 347–374.

Braga, A. (2001). The effects of hot spots policing on crime. *The Annals of the American Academy of Political and Social Science, 578*(November), 104–125.

Braga, A. A. (2005). Hot spots policing and crime prevention: A systematic review of randomized controlled trials. *Journal of Experimental Criminology, 1*(3), 317–342.

Braga, A. A., Weisburd, D. L., Waring, E. J., Mazerolle, L. G., Spelman, W., & Gajewski, F. (1999). Problem-oriented policing in violent crime places: A randomized controlled experiment. *Criminology, 37*(3), 541–580.

Braga, A. A., Papachristos, A. V., & Hureau, D. M. (2014). The effects of hot spots policing on crime: An updated systematic review and meta-analysis. *Justice Quarterly, 31*(4), 633–663.

Braga, A. A., Welsh, B. C., & Schnell, C. (2015). Can policing disorder reduce crime? A systematic review and meta-analysis. *Journal of Research in Crime and Delinquency, 52*(4), 567–588.

Braga, A. A., Turchan, B. S., Papachristos, A. V., & Hureau, D. M. (2019). Hot spots policing and crime reduction: An update of an ongoing systematic review and meta-analysis. *Journal of Experimental Criminology, 15*(3), 289–311.

Buerger, M. E. (1994). The problems of problem solving. *American Journal of Police, 13*(3), 1–36.

Campbell, J. H. (2000). *Keeping illegal activity out of rental property: A police guide for establishing landlord training programs.* U.S. Department of Justice.

Center for Problem-Oriented Policing. (2022). https://popcenter.asu.edu/. Accessed 23 July 2022.

Clarke, R. V. G., & Weisburd, D. (1994). Diffusion of crime control benefits: Observations on the reverse of displacement. In R. V. G. Clarke (Ed.), *Crime prevention studies* (Vol. 2, pp. 165–183). Criminal Justice Press.

Clifton, W., Jr. (1987). *Convenience store robberies in Gainesville, Florida: An intervention strategy by the Gainesville Police Department.* Gainesville Police Department.

Desmond, M., & Valdez, N. (2012). Unpolicing the urban poor: Consequences of third-party policing for inner-city women. *American Sociological Review, 78*(1), 117–141.

Eck, J. E. (1993). The threat of crime displacement. *Criminal Justice Abstracts, 25*(3), 527–546.

Eck, J. E. (1994). *Drug markets and drug places: A case-control study of the spatial structure of illicit drug dealing* (Unpublished doctoral dissertation). University of Maryland College Park.

Eck, J. E. (1997). Do premises liability suits promote business crime prevention? In R. V. Clarke & M. Felson (Eds.), *Business and crime prevention* (pp. 125–150). Criminal Justice Press.

Eck, J. E. (2015). There is nothing so theoretical as good practice: Police-researcher coproduction of place theory. In E. Cochbain & J. Knutsson (Eds.), *Applied police research* (pp. 129–140). Routledge.

Eck, J. E. (2018). Regulation for high-crime places: Theory, evidence, and principles. *The Annals of the American Academy of Political and Social Science, 679*(1), 106–120.

References

Eck, J. E., & Eck, E. B. (2012). Crime place and pollution: Expanding crime reduction options through a regulatory approach. *Criminology & Public Policy, 11*(2), 281–316.

Ellerman, A. D. (2006). Are cap-and-trade programs more environmentally effective than conventional regulations? In J. Freeman & C. D. Kolstad (Eds.), *Moving to markets in environmental regulation: Lessons from twenty years of experience* (pp. 48–62). Oxford University Press.

Frederickson, H. G., & LaPorte, T. R. (2002). Airport security, high reliability, and the problem of rationality. *Public Administration Review, 62*(1), 33–43.

Goldstein, H. (1979). Improving policing: A problem oriented approach. *Crime & Delinquency, 25*(2), 236–258.

Guerette, R. T., & Bowers, K. J. (2009). Assessing the extent of crime displacement and diffusion of benefits: A review of situational crime prevention evaluations. *Criminology, 47*(4), 1331–1368.

Hesseling, R. B. P. (1994). Displacement: A review of the empirical literature. In R. V. Clarke (Ed.), *Crime prevention studies* (Vol. 2, pp. 197–230). Criminal Justice Press.

Hinkle, J. C., Weisburd, D., Telep, C. W., & Petersen, K. (2020). Problem-oriented policing for reducing crime and disorder: An updated systematic review and meta-analysis. *Campbell Systematic Reviews, 16*(2). https://doi.org/10.1002/cl2.1089

Hope, T. (1994). Problem-oriented policing and drug market locations: Three case studies. In R. V. Clarke (Ed.), *Crime prevention studies* (Vol. 2, pp. 5–32). Criminal Justice Press.

Kennedy, D. B., & Hupp, R. T. (1998). Apartment security and litigation: Key issues. *Security Journal, 11*(1), 21–28.

Mazerolle, L. G., & Ransley, J. (2005). *Third party policing*. Cambridge University Press.

Payne, T. C. (2016). Reducing excessive police incidents: Do notices to owners work? *Security Journal, 28*(1), 1–18.

Police Executive Research Forum. (2008). *Violent crime in America: What we know about hot spots enforcement*. Police Executive Research Forum.

Ratcliffe, J. H. (2014). *Schrödinger's crime hotspot*. http://www.jratcliffe/blog/Schrödingers-crime-hotspot

Ratcliffe, J. H., Taniguchi, T., Groff, E. R., & Wood, J. D. (2011). The Philadelphia foot patrol experiment: A randomized controlled trial of police patrol effectiveness in violent crime hot spots. *Criminology, 49*(3), 795–831.

Rosenfeld, R., Deckard, M. J., & Blackburn, E. (2014). The effects of directed patrol and self-initiated enforcement on firearm violence: A randomized controlled study of hot spot policing. *Criminology, 52*(3), 428–449.

Sampson, R. (2007). *False burglar alarms* (Problem specific guide series, no. 5) (2nd ed.). Office of Community Oriented Policing Services.

Santos, R. B., & Santos, R. G. (2016). Offender-focused police intervention in residential burglary and theft from vehicle hot spots: A partially blocked randomized control trial. *Journal of Experimental Criminology, 12*(3), 373–402.

Scott, M. S. (2004). Shifting and sharing police responsibility to address public safety problems. In N. Tilley (Ed.), *Handbook of crime prevention and community safety* (pp. 385–409). Willan.

Sherman, L. W. (1990). Police crackdowns: Initial and residual deterrence. In M. Tonry & N. Morris (Eds.), *Crime and justice: A review of research* (pp. 1–48). University of Chicago Press.

Sherman, L. W., & Rogan, D. P. (1995a). Deterrent effects of police raids on crack houses: A randomized controlled experiment. *Justice Quarterly, 12*(4), 755–782.

Sherman, L. W., & Rogan, D. P. (1995b). Effects of gun seizures on gun violence: 'Hot spots' patrol in Kansas City. *Justice Quarterly, 12*(4), 673–693.

Sherman, L. W., & Weisburd, D. L. (1995). General deterrent effects of police patrol in crime 'hot spots': A randomized controlled trial. *Justice Quarterly, 12*(4), 625–648.

Sparrow, M. K. (2000). *The regulatory craft: Controlling risks, solving problems and managing compliance*. Brookings Institution Press.

Sparrow, M. K. (2008). *The character of harms: Operational challenges in control*. Cambridge University Press.

Weisburd, D. L., & Green, L. (1995). Policing drug hot spots: The Jersey City drug market analysis experiment. *Justice Quarterly, 12*(4), 711–735.

Weisburd, D. L., & Telep, C. W. (2014). Hot spots policing: What we know and what we need to know. *Journal of Contemporary Criminal Justice, 30*(2), 200–220.

Weisburd, D. L., Telep, C. W., Hinkle, J. C., & Eck, J. E. (2010). Is problem-oriented policing effective in reducing crime and disorder? Findings from a Campbell Systematic Review. *Criminology & Public Policy, 9*(1), 139–172.

Worrall, J. L., & Wheeler, A. P. (2019). Evaluating community prosecution code enforcement in Dallas, Texas. *Justice Quarterly, 36*(5), 870–899.

Chapter 10
Rethinking the Forms of Social Control

> *The ownership of land is the great fundamental fact which ultimately determines the social, the political, and consequently the intellectual and moral condition of a people*
>
> – Henry George, Progress and Poverty (1879)

Thinking About Crime and Its Control

Control requires power. The control of mischief and mischief-makers is not an exception. Power may come from a bond between the mischief-maker and a parent. Or power comes from the state. But come power must. This book is about power and control of the serious mischief called crime. It is about a specific source of power and control. The source is so common, so mundane, so unexceptional, and so obvious that most people fail to notice it, or if they notice it, they may fail to see its significance. But you now know better. Unlike you, policy makers and crime researchers usually overlook this source of control. You now know that this source of control is *place management*. And you know why it may be among the most powerful sources of crime control we have.

Having come to the end of this book, you now know why the failure to notice and attend to place management has important consequences. You know that when people attend to place management, they can reduce crime, and when they fail to address place management, their policies are often unsustainable, usually costly, and frequently ineffective.

You now know the facts. Crime is concentrated at a very small proportion of addresses. Most addresses in any neighborhood have little or no crime. A few addresses, in any neighborhood, have a great deal of crime. There are many explanations for these two facts; all involve the way owners and operators use their property rights to manage their places. Most place managers exercise their property rights in ways that keep their places safe. Public policy should build on these successes. A few place managers fail persistently. These few persistent failures create much of the crime neighborhoods experience. To control crime, public policy must reverse these routine failures.

You now know that safety is not created just by police or just by community residents or by some combination. Place managers exercise considerable control over people's behaviors. And place managers are not police and they often are not residents. Their influence can extend beyond their property into surrounding areas. Understanding place management reveals effective crime control strategies that can reduce the use of criminal sanctions, strategies with teeth so the police do not have to bite as often or as hard.

In the previous chapter, you saw our options for reducing crime at high-crime places. Given the hockey stick shape of crime, if these policies drive down crime at the hottest proprietary places (i.e., the blade) and within their purlieus, then cities that use these policies should see reductions in crime.

In this chapter, we consider how we think about crime. How we think about crime shapes policy. Useful ideas can create in policies that save lives, prevent injury, reduce property theft, curtail property damage, and promote feelings of security and safety. Useless ideas result in none of these.

The Problems of Neighborhood Thinking

Our book is about proprietary places, not pooled places such as neighborhoods. Nevertheless, we need to discuss how proprietary places fit within neighborhoods because policy makers and researchers often imagine crime as a neighborhood problem.

One of the biggest problems discussing neighborhoods is that the term is ambiguous (Baffoe, 2019; Galster, 2001; Martin, 2003; Wilcox et al., 2018). It has at least five meanings, which people often confuse. Each meaning generates a different set of neighborhood boundaries. A neighborhood can be:

1. A *geographic subdivision* useful for organizing data. Census tracts, in the United States, are statistical neighborhoods.
2. An *administrative subdivision* drawn by an organization to help it do its work. Examples of administrative neighborhoods include police districts, electoral precincts, zip and postal code areas, school catchment areas, church parishes, and other service areas.
3. A *market area* for the sales of goods and services. Real estate agents divide cities to enhance the buying and selling of properties. Developers create blocks of housing, centers for shopping, and industrial parks.
4. A *political subdivision* to help residents express their interests and power. Examples include wards represented by city council members, state representative districts, or a riding (in British Commonwealth countries).
5. A *natural community* of people who live near each other and who interact to influence the social order of their common area.

In first four meanings, an institution drew boundaries to serve its purposes: neighborhood is a means to the institution's ends. The people who live within these neighborhoods did not define the boundaries. Residents adapt to the boundaries or they ignore them.

The fifth meaning is different. The neighborhood is not a means to an institution's end. No one planned it or intentionally created it. Instead, residents made decisions individually, came together, and found common interests. In doing so, they unwittingly created a superorganism, the community that has intent and abilities greater than all its members. In North America, a homeless encampment might be such a neighborhood, assuming no public or private organization established it (Speer, 2017). In other parts of the world, squatter communities might qualify as neighborhoods of this type (Neuwirth, 2006).

When researchers use this fifth meaning, a neighborhood is *a functioning entity with its own goals and abilities*: goals and abilities distinct from the goals and abilities of the people who use the area. It is this meaning that animates much talk of community-based crime control and social order. Its foundation is in the 100-year tradition of social disorganization theory (Park, 1925/1967; Shaw & McKay, 1942/1972).

Collective efficacy (Sampson et al., 1997) and broken windows (Wilson & Kelling, 1982), two of the most prominent of the neighborhood theories (Wilcox et al., 2018), imagine type 5 neighborhoods. Both theories use community and neighborhood interchangeably. Both propose that order and safety are goals of all neighborhoods as illustrated in these quotes (emphasis added):

> ...social control refers generally to the *capacity of a group* to regulate its members according to desired principles–to realize collective, as opposed to forced, goals (Sampson et al., 1997, p. 918).

> The essence of the police role in maintaining order is to reinforce the informal control mechanisms of the *community itself*. The police cannot, without committing extraordinary resources, provide a substitute for that informal control. On the other hand, to reinforce those natural forces the police must accommodate them (Wilson & Kelling, 1982, p. 34).

These and other community theories share the neighborhood resident emergent control (NREC) framework (Linning et al., 2022a). They all focus on the fifth kind of *neighborhoods*, not proprietary or proximal places. They all assume *residents* are the most important actors, maybe the only actors, for addressing crime. They all assume it's the collective action of residents that *control* crime. Finally, they all are *emergent;* these controls arise from within the neighborhood, organically, naturally, and without plans or directions from outside.

Proprietary places create neighborhoods

Neighborhoods are not useful units for reducing crime and increasing safety. Focusing on proprietary places may be more effective.

Theories embracing the NREC framework claim that the controls needed to keep crime down emerge from the numerous daily encounters area residents have with each other. The neighborhood is an organism. As Robert Sampson and W. Byron Groves (1989: p. 777) stated, "social disorganization refers to the inability of a community structure to realize the common values of its residents and maintain effective social control." When this organism loses its ability to achieve its goal, it is disorganized. The goals, and abilities, are not the goals or abilities of individual residents, just as the goals and abilities of your body's cells are not the same as your goals and abilities.

Imagine a neighborhood where these encounters, and the personal connections these encounters produce, create shared expectations about what is appropriate behavior. Moreover, they give rise to shared expectations about what residents should do about inappropriate behaviors they see. Then, when they see signs of trouble, they will act. Residents' many small informal social acts keep crime down.

Now imagine a second neighborhood, where residents disagree about what is good and bad behavior. They are unable or unwilling to intervene to deal with trouble. Their neighborhood will have a great deal of crime for want of informal social control. No residents like crime, yet the second neighborhood has a lot of it and the first neighborhood has little.

The NREC framework rests on three assumptions, each false. The first assumption is that neighborhoods are natural; their boundaries arose through the unregulated movement of people and the unguided economics of housing markets. In reality, most recognizable neighborhoods are creations of people from outside the neighborhood: subdivisions created by developers, housing projects created by public housing agencies, concentrated racial enclaves created by historic discrimination, and other institutions operating in their interests (Linning & Eck, 2021). When we see very similar housing stock, built about the same time, we are seeing the fossil footprints of neighborhood developers. When we see grid street patterns, we are seeing the trace evidence of city planners, engineers, and developers. When we encounter zoning requirements, we see evidence of past political decisions about who can do what where (Linning et al., 2022a).

The second assumption is that residents matter most; they are the actors who create or fail to create informal social control. Throughout this book, we described how place managers, exercising their property rights, create order at their places and between places. The NREC framework fails to account for place management control. If all neighborhoods consisted only of single-family homeowners, then overlooking place management would not matter because all adult residents would be place managers of their homes. Because most neighborhoods contain both property owners and residents, some of whom do not own property, place management varies within and between neighborhoods.

When neighborhood residents rent, they are often renting from people based outside of their neighborhood. This is particularly true of low-income neighborhoods where home ownership is low compared to other neighborhoods. It is certainly true in public housing. In low-income areas, many of the people with the power to make changes that influence crime live outside the area. The people who live with crime usually do not have these powers so they are forced to adapt to the environments created by those that do (Linning et al., 2022a).

The third NREC assumption is that social forces (so-called structural factors like area wealth versus poverty, residential stability versus turnover, population homogeneity versus diversity) create conditions that encourage or impede the emergence of informal social control. NREC treats these structural factors as acts of nature, like weather. However, lending institutions, businesses, and governments create much of what helps or hinders residents (Linning et al., 2022a).

In John's area, for example, a developer bought a former insurance company office complex, tore it down, and constructed over 300 market rate rental units and a dozen street-level shops. The developer's decision will have a large impact on the people who live near John. The developer's decisions persuaded the city to alter the local road network. These alterations influence where people drive and walk. The influx of young affluent renters will precipitate other businesses to choose to locate in the area. The demand for housing in the area will increase, driving up property taxes and rents, which may force some lower-income, long-term residents to move elsewhere. All of these choices, mostly by people and organizations based outside John's neighborhood, will change the structural factors and crime patterns in his area. Some changes will cost local residents and some changes will benefit them (we gave other examples of how outsiders can help create safety in Chap. 8). The important lesson is that structural factors do not naturally occur like the tides, ocean currents, and rainbows; people and institutions shape them.

In contrast to the NREC framework, our thesis is that order comes from proprietary place management. Place managers establish order within their locations and attempt to radiate order into their surroundings. Some of these place managers are residents, but many are not. We are skeptical of the fifth notion of neighborhood embraced by NREC.

Proprietary places create neighborhoods, so we call our alternative the *Neighborhood Out of Places Explanation* (NOPE) (Linning et al., 2022a). NOPE does not make residents' actions the explanation for most crime. Instead, NOPE points to the small number of locations where crime is the highest and to the people who own and operate these places. Social forces like wealth and poverty and residential mobility may assist or hinder place management. That is why so-called structural factors are correlated with crime. Residents' collective action may have some influence on minor disorders, but the more serious the crime, the less influence informal social control is likely to have. Residents matter, however, because they can act politically. It is their political actions, not their everyday social interactions, that carry weight in the battles against crime.

We suggest researchers go back to the insights of Charles Booth and W. E. Du Bois and examine crime variation among property parcels. Without accounting for place-based crime causes, it is not productive for researchers and policy makers to consider neighborhood causes.

Forms of Control

Is place management the sole form of nongovernment control of crime? Of course not. But dwelling on residents' abilities to forge community order overlooks a pervasive and obvious source of control. Try this experiment yourself. Stroll through any neighborhood, going into as many shops, restaurants, bars, salons, churches, schools, apartment buildings, and single-family homes as you can. Make a note of all the times you witness someone informally controlling someone (outside of their family). Note all the times you witness the police controlling someone. And make a note all the signs of place management control. You will find that the evidence of place management controls is greater than the evidence of the other two types. This experiment does not show that place management control is more powerful. But it does show that it is everywhere and it is not hidden.

Criminologists should abandon the formal versus informal social control dichotomy. It was a useful discussion point once. Now the distinction impedes progress (Linning et al., 2022b). We propose an alternative classification of control, keeping some of the ideas in the old dichotomy but adding more details.

Figure 10.1 shows the structure of our proposal. Instead of two forms of control, there are at least four. Why *at least*? Because we are not claiming we have described all forms of controls and we want researchers to look for others.

Forms of Control

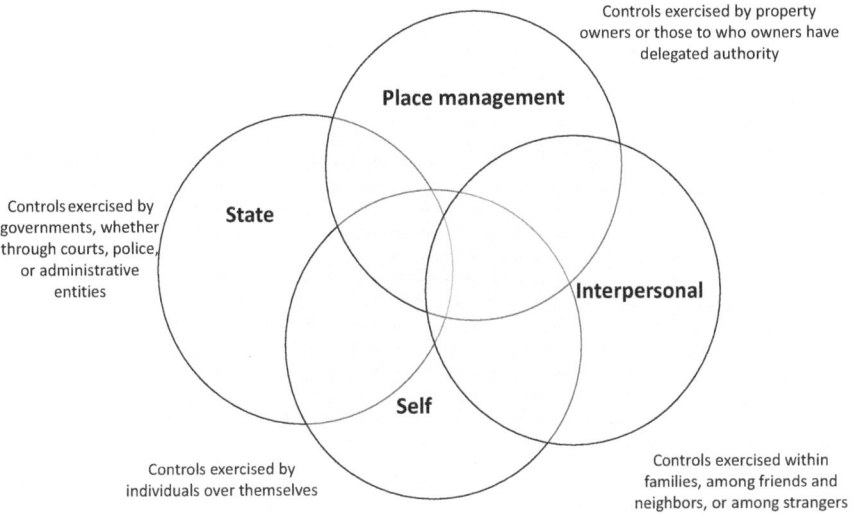

Fig. 10.1 Forms of control

State Control

We abandon the vague term *formal* and replace it with its clearer synonym. Within *state* control are all forms of control imposed by government actors: police, prosecution, courts, corrections, regulatory agencies, and so forth. If a state-run bureaucracy exerts this control, then it is state control. This means that calling the police is a form of state control (but we will say more about this later).

Place Management

We have discussed this form of control at length. This is control exerted by actors based on their property rights. Proprietary place owners (including homeowners), or people and organizations to whom owners have delegated authority, exert place *management* control. We have shown that such delegation can come through employment, rental and lease agreements, contracts, and other legal agreements.

We have described how place managers express their control by organizing physical space. Place managers express their control by regulating place user conduct. Place managers express their control by regulating access. Finally, place managers express their control by the ways they derive their resources.

Self-Control

The controls we put on ourselves are *self-control*: not hitting people who insulted us, not taking things that tempt us, not acting wildly when the setting provokes us. It is the control of our impulsive urges, and it is delayed gratification (Gottfredson & Hirschi, 1990).

Interpersonal Control

Most of what was called informal social control fits here. We suggest at least three types: families, friends, and strangers. Within families, members control each other using inducements and sanctions. Friends and acquaintances control each other with other forms of inducements and sanctions. Moreover, strangers can control each other, but not in same way that families or friends do. Within crowds, for example, people mimic the behavior of those around them to fit in (McPhail, 1991). The sources of power for these three types of interpersonal control may be very different. If they are very different, we recommend abandoning our umbrella category of interpersonal control. We would then have six forms of control: state, place management, self, family, friends, and strangers.

Overlaps and Layers

Controls overlap, as Fig. 10.1 implies. A government, for example, exercises place management over its property. Place managers may try to encourage self-control or interpersonal control. When a person calls the police, she initiates state control. The state encourages these calls with public announcements, technology, and procedures. A person with suicidal urges may call 911 for help: self-control overlapping with state control.

We should recognize that, to some degree, the controls are interchangeable. If one fails, people shift to using another. If family members or neighbors cannot agree (interpersonal control), they may call the police (state control). A bartender may try to expel a rowdy drunk (place management), but fail. She calls the police to remove him (state control). When a city had trouble maintaining order at an annual gathering (state control), it turned the event over to a private operation (place management control) (Plant & Scott, 2011). Imagine that a court (state control) orders a drug offender to undertake rehabilitation at a private clinic. While at the clinic, the client is under place management, until he can learn to exercise greater control over his life (self-control). Just before release from the clinic, the staff works with the client's family so they can support the client (interpersonal control).

Seen this way, we see control not as one type or another. Instead, control is a layered defense against crime and disorder. If one layer is weak, or fails, people call upon other layers to continue to provide protection. The layers reinforce each other: for example, it may be easier for people to exercise self-control when they know others are watching, there are clear rules, and that consequences will follow rule breaking.

Controls as layered defenses make sense given that each type of control has its own power source: government for state, property rights for place management, desire to belong to groups for interpersonal, and thought processing for self-control. A failure of one layer usually does not create a cascade of failures through all layers. Also, the costs of each layer are different depending on how one looks at the defense. From a social perspective, self-control may be the least expensive and state control the most expensive. However, from the perspective of a place manager, self and interpersonal controls may appear the least costly: followed by state control, with place management control the most costly. For some individuals, it may be less costly to be controlled from outside than to exert self-control: the drunk who depends on the bartender to cut him off and his friends to drive him home.

Four Questions

By expanding the categories, being more attentive to the sources of power, and allowing for transfers of control across categories, crime researchers can develop a richer understanding of how we maintain order. These changes also make policy decisions clearer. Rather than abstract debates over which is more useful or ideologically pure, policy makers can examine which forms of control are available and which need to be bolstered to create order. The mix of controls will vary from place to place and over time. Nevertheless, at any place, place management must be a central concern.

Making place management control obvious avoids asking residents or police to do things they are incapable of doing. In an apartment building beset by package theft from the foyer, for example, the owner can apply situational prevention techniques, but the residents cannot. Moreover, because place management is highly circumscribed by place boundaries, drawing on place management helps avoid over control. In many circumstances, place managers can find solutions that work and work rather quickly. We cannot say this about interpersonal controls as we have yet to find reliable ways of injecting these into communities.

Implicitly, we recognize the value of place management when we tackle Internet crimes. If a social network or other web platform permits users to post statements advocating violence, sell illicit drugs, sell stolen goods, traffic humans, or engage in other criminal activity, we do not blame this on a breakdown of informal social control. Nor is our primary line of defense our local police service. Rather, we demand the owners and operators of the platforms to exercise controls. It is the owners and operators of Internet platforms who designed the sites and have the powers necessary to make useful changes (Baughan, 2021; Katyal, 2003; KnujOn, 2012; Llinares & Johnson, 2018). With regard to things on the Internet, we recognize that people and organizations create opportunities for crime and can create opportunities for safety.

It is odd that something as diffuse and global as the Internet teaches us lessons about discreet local places. However, in both cases ownership and control matter. In both cases ownership and control often are located far from where crimes occur. And in both cases, the everyday user has little power to change the environment.

We need to make place management visible. We need to see its everyday powers. We need to attend to controls place managers can use to make us safer. If we attend to place management, we see that much crime is hyperlocal and that it is the breakdowns of controls at very small spots that are responsible for much of the trouble. Attending to place management means asking four questions and acting on the answers. (1) *Where* precisely is crime the highest? (2) *Who* owns or operates these proprietary places? (3) *How* do their management practices create crime conditions? (4) *What* can be done to get the managers of these places to change their practices so that crime declines? You should ask these four questions and act on the answers.

References

Baffoe, G. (2019). Understanding the neighborhood concept and its evolution: A review. *Environment and Urbanization ASIA, 10*(2), 393–402.

Baughan, A. (2021). Toxic online disagreements are largely due to social media design. *The Next Web*. https://thenextweb.com/news/toxic-online-disagreements-social-media-design-%0Asyndication?utm_medium=tech.auto.fri.20210709&utm_source=email&utm_content=&utm_campaign=campaign%0A

Galster, G. (2001). On the nature of neighbourhood. *Urban Studies, 38*(12), 2111–2124.

Gottfredson, M., & Hirschi, T. (1990). *A general theory of crime*. Stanford University Press.

Katyal, N. K. (2003). Digital architecture as crime control. *The Yale Law Journal, 112*(8), 2261–2289.

KnujOn. (2012). *Rogue domain registrars – 1st quarter 2012: A deep review of illicit internet drug traffic and ICANN policy*. KnujOn. Archived on Wayback Machine. https://web.archive.org/web/20190402091254/http://www.knujon.com/rogue_registrars_2012.pdf. Accessed 22 Aug 2022.

Linning, S. J., & Eck, J. E. (2021). *Whose 'eyes on the street' control crime?* Cambridge University Press.

Linning, S. J., Olaghere, A., & Eck, J. E. (2022a). Say NOPE to social disorganization criminology: The importance of creators in neighborhood social control. *Crime Science, 11*(5), 1–11. https://doi.org/10.1186/s40163-022-00167-y

Linning, S. J., Olaghere, A., Eck. J. E., & Steinman, H. (2022b, November 16). *What is informal social control? A review of the criminology literature, 2010–2020*. Presentation at the conference of the American Society of Criminology, Atlanta, GA.

Llinares, F. M., & Johnson, S. D. (2018). Cybercrime and place: Applying environmental criminology to crimes in cyberspace. In G. J. N. Bruinsma & S. D. Johnson (Eds.), *The Oxford handbook of environmental criminology* (pp. 883–906). Oxford University Press.

Martin, D. G. (2003). Enacting neighborhood. *Urban Geography, 24*(5), 361–385.

References

McPhail, C. (1991). *The myth of the madding crowd*. Aldine.

Neuwirth, R. (2006). *Shadow cities: A billion squatters, a new urban world*. Routledge.

Park, R. E. (1925/1967). Community organization and juvenile delinquency. In R. E. Park, E. W. Burgess, & R. D. McKenzie (Eds.), *The city* (pp. 99–112). University of Chicago Press.

Plant, J. B., & Scott, M. S. (2011). Trick or treat? Policing Halloween in Madison, Wisconsin. In T. D. Madensen & J. Knutsson (Eds.), *Preventing crowd violence* (pp. 159–190). Lynne Rienner Publishers.

Sampson, R. J., & Groves, W. B. (1989). Community structure and crime: Testing social-disorganization theory. *The American Journal of Sociology, 94*(4), 774–802.

Sampson, R. J., Raudenbush, S. W., & Earls, F. (1997). Neighborhoods and violent crime: A multilevel study of collective efficacy. *Science, 277*(5328), 918–924.

Shaw, C. R., & McKay, H. D. (1942/1972). *Juvenile delinquency and urban areas: A study of rates of delinquency in relation to differential characteristics of local communities in American cities* (Revised ed.). University of Chicago Press.

Speer, J. (2017). 'It's not like your home:' Homeless encampments, housing projects, and the struggle over domestic space. *Antipode, 49*(2), 517–535.

Wilcox, P., Cullen, F. T., & Feldmeyer, B. (2018). *Communities and crime: An enduring American challenge*. Temple University Press.

Wilson, J. Q., & Kelling, G. L. (1982). Broken windows: The police and neighborhood safety. *The Atlantic Monthly, 249*(3), 29–38.

Index

A
Abt, T., 72
Acquisition of resources, 27, 40, 48
Agglomeration economies, 82
Americans with Disabilities Act, 39
Andresen, M.A., 12, 59

B
Bichler, G., 69
Booth, C., 3, 5, 106
Boulder, 13
Bowers, K., 62, 63
Braga, A.A., 17, 89, 90
Brantingham, P.J., 13, 15, 59
Brantingham, P.L., 13, 15, 59
Buffers, 55–59
Bundle of Rights, 38–41
Bundle of sticks, *see* Bundle of rights
Business improvement districts (BIDs) ambassadors, 84

C
Chula Vista (California), 13, 95
Cincinnati (Ohio), 7, 19, 59, 67, 68, 73, 75, 76, 79, 83, 85, 86
Civil litigation, 85, 94
Clarke, R.V., 7, 14, 17, 29–31, 61, 90
Cleveland (Ohio), 57
Comfort spaces, 68, 70, 73, 74
Command and control, 93, 96
Confidential informants, 74

Control of access, 27, 31, 39
Convergence settings, 69, 70, 73, 74
Corrupting spots, 70, 71, 73, 74
Crime anchor points, 61, 62
Crime attractors, 15
Crime generators, 13, 29
Crime-involved place, 64, 67–77, 92, 97
Crime prevention through environmental design (CPTED), 17, 25, 39
Crime sites, 63, 69, 70, 72, 74, 76
Crime-sucking places, 61
CS^4, 71, 72

D
Dallas (Texas), 76
Defensible space, 17, 25, 39
Denver (Colorado), 76
Diffusion of benefits, 61, 91
Displacement of crime, 61
Du Bois, W.E.B., 4–6, 106

E
Edmonton (Alberta), 57
Enablers, 46
Ends, 2, 11, 18, 19, 27, 34, 71, 80, 93–96, 101, 103
Enriquez, J., 69
Eybergen, C., 59
Eyes
  constant succession of, 79, 80, 86
  on the street, 16, 79, 80, 82, 86

F
Federal Housing Administration (FHA), 85
Felson, M., 11, 16
Formal control, 33, 46

G
Goldstein, H., 75, 91
Groff, E.R., 5, 19, 34–36
Groves, W.B., 14, 104
Guardians, 11, 16, 18, 24, 28, 45, 46, 80
Guardianship, 16, 17, 24, 28, 31, 33, 35, 42, 80, 84

H
Hammer, M., 68, 70, 76
Handlers, 11, 16, 18, 24, 45, 46
Herman Goldstein Award, 75
Herold, M., 67, 68, 71–73, 76
Hidden crime places, 68, 71, 72, 74
Hipp, J.R., 36
Hockey stick, 7, 8, 11, 13–15, 17, 18, 30, 52, 53, 59, 69, 79, 95, 102
Honore', A.M., 38–40
Hot spots
 patrols, 89–91, 97
Hunter, R., 4

I
Informal social control, 17, 19, 28, 33–37, 42, 43, 76, 104–106, 108, 109
Infrastructures, 71, 72, 74, 76
Interpersonal controls, 108, 109

J
Jacobs, J., 16, 79, 80, 82, 84, 86
Jeffery, C.R., 17

K
Kelling, G.L., 103

L
Land uses, 7, 80
Lee, Y., 7, 14, 15, 19, 60

M
MacDonald, J., 59
Magnetic locations, 69

Magnet phones, 13
Malm, A., 69
Manager network, 86
Means, 2, 3, 31, 34, 37, 52, 61, 80, 81, 85, 86, 93–96, 103, 107, 110
Minneapolis (Minnesota), 4, 5, 7, 12, 57, 90
Moyer, R.A., 59

N
Neighborhood Out of Places Explanation (NOPE), 106
Neighborhood Resident Emergent Control (NREC), 103–105
Neighborhoods, 1–8, 17, 19, 20, 33, 37, 41, 42, 50, 55–57, 68, 71, 72, 74, 76, 83–86, 101–106
Newcastle upon Tyne (United Kingdom)
Newman, O., 17, 18

O
ORCA, 24, 27, 34, 40–42
Organization of space, 25, 27, 31
Ostrom, E., 38–40

P
Perrow, C., 46, 48, 49
Philadelphia (Pennsylvania), 4, 57, 76
Place management, 1–3, 8, 11, 19, 20, 23–25, 27, 28, 31, 33, 34, 36, 37, 39–43, 46, 59, 76, 80, 85, 86, 91, 101, 102, 105–110
Place managers, 1, 3, 8, 16, 20, 23–34, 37, 39–43, 45–53, 55–64, 67–77, 79–87, 89, 91–94, 96, 97, 101, 102, 105, 107–110
Place network
 board (PNI), 74, 75
 investigations (PNI), 68, 75, 76, 92
Pooled places, 5, 6, 68, 102
Problem-oriented policing, 75, 89, 91, 92, 97
Problem-solving, 90–92, 98
Promoters, 46
Property rights, 1, 37–38, 40–43, 101, 105, 107, 109
Proprietary places, 2–8, 11, 12, 17, 19, 20, 23, 27, 48, 49, 55, 68–70, 72, 91, 92, 97, 102, 105–107, 110
Proximal places, 5–7, 17, 19, 20, 103
Purlieu, 55–57, 61, 91

R

Racial covenants, 41, 42
Radiation, 55–64, 67, 86
Ratcliffe, J.H., 55, 57–59, 90
Reactors, 46
Regulation of conduct, 27, 29, 31, 39
Regulations, 26, 28–29, 39, 40, 46, 48, 85, 87, 89, 92–97
Repeat offenders, 16
Repeat victimization, 14, 28
Reynald, D.M., 24, 35
Ridgeway, G., 59
Risky facilities, 7
Routine activity theory, 11, 18, 31

S

Sampson, R.J., 35, 36, 46, 104
San Diego (California), 57
Schlaeger, E., 38–40
Self-control, 108, 109
Shelley v. Kraemer, 42
Sherman, L.W., 4, 5, 7, 12, 90, 91
Situational crime prevention, 17, 25, 29–31, 39
Sparrow, M., 92
State control, 107–109
Sticky, 72, 76
Subsidies, 49, 94, 96
Super controllers, 45–48, 52, 53, 75, 85
Suppressors, 46

T

Tradable permits, 95
Tucson (Arizona), 76

W

Weisburd, D., 3, 5, 6, 19, 61, 90
Wichita (Kansas), 76
Wickes, R., 35, 36
Wilcox, P., 7, 19
Wilson, J.Q., 103

Y

Yang, S.-M., 5, 6, 19

Z

Zidar, M., 13, 29

The manufacturer's authorised representative in the EU is Springer Nature Customer Service Centre GmbH, Europaplatz 3, 69115 Heidelberg, Germany. If you have any concerns regarding our products, please contact ProductSafety@springernature.com

Printed and bound by CPI Group (UK) Ltd, Croydon, CR0 4YY
23/03/2026
02076398-0016